Born out of frustration and despair,
This is Belgium is first and foremost
a love and hate affair.

Inside Spa-Francorchamps

The scene of many legendary races – one of the most memorable being Mika Häkkinen's infamous overtake of Michael Schumacher in the final laps of the Formula One Belgian Grand Prix in 2000 – Spa Francorchamps, at just over 7km long, sits in between the Belgian towns of Spa, Malmedy and Stavelot. Notorious amongst drivers for its deadly corners and tricky turns (over 45 drivers and 4 officials have lost their lives here), it is also one of their favourites. Indeed, with a reputation for fast, winding and hilly drives, unpredictable weather patterns and one of the most breathtaking settings in the world of Formula One racing, Spa Francorchamps remains one of the few racetracks that continue to challenge drivers' skill and technique.

4   Inside Spa-Francorchamps

12   Inside Knokke

16   Best for emerging art

32   Pietro Celestina on Antwerp's 2060 district

34   Dirk Braeckman on Ghent Zuid

36   Best for photography

46   Iconic Belgian photography books

48   Best for art books

58   Inside R.S.C.Anderlecht

62   Iconic Belgian films

64   Best for arthouse cinema

74   Kaat Debo on Antwerp's 2000 district

76   Best for city views

82   Iconic Belgian records

84   Best for records

Robert Heinecken

Lessons in Posing Subjects

WIELS

Av. Van Volxemlaan 354
1190 Brussels
www.wiels.org

The exhibition is generously sponsored by the galleries Cherry and Martin, Petzel, Marc Selwyn Fine Art and Rhona Hoffman

100	Nosedrip on Ostend
102	Best for live music
118	A weekend getaway at L'Ardoisière
120	Best for vintage design
128	Marie Pok on Wallonia & Brussels' design scenes
130	Dieter Van Den Storm on Brussels' North district
132	Charly Wittock on Brussels landmarks
136	Belgium's street artists
142	Belgium's hidden celebrity sightings
144	What the people really want
146	Devrim Bayar on Brussels' art scene
148	Murielle Scherre on Ghent
150	Best for fountains in Brussels
154	Here, there and everywhere

TRANCHES DE VIE
SOFIE LACHAERT + LUC D'HANIS

GRAND-HORNU IMAGES
27/04 > 17/08 2014

SITE DU GRAND-HORNU - RUE SAINTE-LOUISE - 7301 HORNU, BELGIUM
+32 (0) 65 65 21 21 - WWW.GRAND-HORNU-IMAGES.BE
OPEN FROM TUESDAY TO SUNDAY FROM 10.00 TO 18.00

Inside Knokke

Like Ostend or Nieuwpoort, Knokke is a typical Belgian coastal town in the sense that a great number of families have for generations owned second homes here. Unlike other towns however, and due in part to the Lippens family's iron-fisted rule on Knokke's fiscal policies and real estate developments, it attracts a certain breed of Belgian family. Think Sunday parades of luxury sports cars, SUVs and golf carts alongside the town's Croisette. Although here it's called L'Avenue du Littoral. Beyond its reputation as a bling magnet though, Knokke also rates high with Belgian families who come here to surf, play golf or go for kilometre-long walks in Het Zwin, the nearby nature reserve.

Best for
emerging
art

EXTRA CITY

25 Eikelstraat (2600)
extracitykunsthal.org

ANTWERP

LLS 387

387 Lange Leemstraat (2018)
users.telenet.be/lls387

ANTWERP

Founded in 2004 by curator and critic Wim Peeters, Antwerp's Extra City started out in an unheated space down at the docks. Now they've set up in a large industrial building in Antwerp's cool Zuid area. Renovations have just been completed and the centre now includes an enormous exhibition space on several floors and even a small cinema. "We want to be a hub and platform for the local scene and at the same time connect it to international developments in contemporary art," explains the centre's current artistic director, Romanian-born Mihnea Mircan.

Austrian-born art critic Ulrike Lindmayr founded the non-profit art space LLS 387 in 2007. "I try to organise projects that are possible *because* we're on the periphery, not despite it," Ulrike says. Collaborations and promoting young emerging artists are priorities: for the exhibition NowBelgiumNow Ulrike travelled the country with Stella Lohaus to visit 90 artists in order to choose nine of them for the exhibition. LLS 387 unites professionalism and experience with an alternative approach and improvisation: "The small budget we have keeps us on our feet."

LOKAAL01
287 Provinciestraat (2018)
lokaal01.nl

ANTWERP

OBJECTIF EXHIBITIONS
7-9/26 Kleine Markt (2000)
objectif-exhibitions.org

ANTWERP

Originally founded as a branch of the gallery of the same name located in the Dutch city of Breda, the Antwerp sister-venue is now the only location for the franchise, which every year offers residencies with exhibitions to artists from all over the world, the idea being to support young artists. "Applicants have to make a proposal that relates to the Antwerp space – other than that there are no rules," says artistic director Frederik Vergaert. Five or six artists are selected annually to work at Lokaal01 for about four weeks, where they prepare their final exhibition pieces.

Since its founding in 1999, non-profit Objectif Exhibitions has stayed true to its original concept, which is to offer a small, flexible space that operates at the edges of contemporary art, with an eclectic programme and a prolific number of shows per year. Every four years the artistic director changes and it is currently headed by New York-born Chris Fitzpatrick: "I try to organise the shows in a way that they overlap with each other in order to create conversations between different artists," he explains. Objectif Exhibitions is open to all genres and practices, and one of its most recent shows included the video works of Raphael Montañez Ortiz.

SECONDROOM
30 Ijzerlaan (2060)
secondroom-antwerpen.tumblr.com

ABILENE GALLERY
163 Rue de la Victoire
/ Overwinningsstraat (1060)
abilenegallery.com

When SECONDroom first appeared in September 2006, it was located in a spare room of co-founder Christophe Floré's Brussels house. Three years ago he moved to Antwerp and took the concept with him. Now, he and his colleagues organise shows at a rate of about one a week. It's an unusually high frequency, and they've clocked hundreds of exhibitions to date. "Our motto is: cut the crap," says Christophe. Visitors can only see the artworks for about three hours at the opening reception, which is also the closing event. Exhibited artists range from emerging to established.

One of the precursors to the small influx of art spaces coming to the city's Saint-Gilles/Sint-Gillis neighbourhood over the past two years, Abilene is a space whose focus lies in contemporary creation in its broadest sense. With a roster of activities that includes exhibitions (some of which are conceived in the basement's workshop), performances, publications and concerts, the space's founders insist on it as an incubator for all types of initiatives. "We want to be a platform where people meet, and transform that energy into exhibitions, concerts and performances – anything conceivable," say the founders, who all met at the entrance exam at La Cambre. They've since succeeded in bringing the art-going masses a little further south on opening night.

CAB

32-34 Rue Borrensstraat (1050)
cab.be

DE LA CHARGE

152 Rue Théodore Verhaegenstraat (1060)
delacharge.com

Contemporary Art Brussels was founded in 2012 by businessman Hubert Bonnet, who was initially trying to find somewhere to store his own art collection. This industrial-looking 1930s art deco warehouse and former dance hall, set a stone's throw from Ixelles's hospital, features abundant natural light and hosts guest curators for themed Belgian and international shows. There are two major projects per year, and recent sample shows have included 'Bande à Part' which marked close collaborator Baronian Gallery's 40th anniversary and featured highlights from Belgium's art scene, while 'Pionnières' featured renowned female artists such as Tracey Emin, Linda Benglis and Louise Bourgeois.

Because of its rather large number of participating artists – a total of 19 are linked to the space – De La Charge is probably the closest Brussels gets to Andy Wharol's Factory – at least in terms of sheer energy. Dominated by a dramatic staircase around which most of the artists' own private areas are housed, the atypical house's many different zones make it perfectly suited to artistic freedom and creative projects of all sorts, which also partly helps to explain its *laissez-faire* approach to programming. "Everyone here can suggest a show," says member Martin Belou. "We're open to everything and never veto proposals." With the stated purpose of giving young and emerging artists of all disciplines a window to showcase their work, De La Charge sits at the rather more experimental and untested end of the spectrum.

ÉTABLISSEMENT D'EN FACE

32 Rue Ravensteinstraat (1000)

etablissementdenfaceprojects.org

ISLAND

32 Chaussée de Wavre
/ Waversesteenweg (1000)

islandisland.be

The first artist-run space in Brussels, Établissement d'en Face is managed by artist Harald Thys and Margot Vanheusden (also of NICC), who run the space with a tight-knit group of volunteers. A firm fixture on the local art scene, it was founded in 1991 and has been showing both emerging and established artists ever since. "We don't have any particular criteria when choosing the artist, and decide from project to project," says co-founder Etienne Wynants, who stresses the non-commercial interest of the project: "We never choose someone because they sell well." Recent projects have included an exhibition by Lou Ford, the space's yearly awards for best works seen (cutely named Les Pots d'Etablissement) as well as the launch of Michael, Belgian artists David De Tscharner and Benoit Plateus' latest edition.

Located at the start of Brussels' bustling African quarter of Matonge, right beside the excellent wine bar Titulus, Island is one of the city's most recent openings. Established and run by local artists Sébastien Bonin and Brice Guilbert, the space's highbrow and cerebral programme includes solo exhibitions, group shows as well as talks, which all take place in the gallery's intimate setting. Opening nights are always a fun-filled family affair and the limited amount of square metres means crowds never fail to spill out onto the street.

THE ISTER

42 Rue Vandenbrandenstraat (1000)
theister.be

KOMPLOT

295 Avenue Van Volxemlaan (1190)
kmplt.be

The Ister was founded in late 2011 by a tight-knit tribe of eight friends from backgrounds as diverse as theatre, production, food and neuroscience. An itinerant art project that is highly personal in its choices, The Ister suggests a range of alternating projects, from dinners and performances to workshops and talks, all in different forms and each with different functions. Turning up at many major art world happenings in London, Berlin, Paris and Brussels, The Ister is a natural extension of its founders' evolving interests. "We prefer having to reinvent ourselves constantly; it's much more exciting and enriching," says co-founder Lila Pérès.

A firm favourite on the local circuit since its opening in 2002, Brussels' Komplot is one of the more established non-profit art spaces in the Belgian capital. An art centre run by a collective of curators, Komplot "looks like a gallery but it isn't one," says co-founder Sonia Dermience. Housed in a large space just a few steps from WIELS (Brussels' Centre for Contemporary Art), it features exhibition rooms (one of which is a former garage space), 10 artist studios as well as a few rooms it uses for its residency programme. A multidisciplinary platform in the truest sense, Komplot embraces both visual artists and writers, organises projects abroad, publishes a magazine called YEAR and also organises the yearly independent publishing showcase Artists Prints together with JAP, the latest edition of which took place in March 2014.

LA LOGE

86 Rue de l'Ermitage Kluisstraat (1050)
la-loge.be

BRUSSELS

MIDDLEMARCH

550 Chaussée de Waterloo
/ Waterloosesteenweg (1050)
middlemarch.be

BRUSSELS

Set in a former Masonic temple nestled on the upper side of Ixelles/Elsene's Flagey district, La Loge is a privately-funded non-profit art space that puts on close to five exhibitions a year. Established in 2011 by architect Philippe Rotthier, its current Director Anne-Claire Schmitz describes it as being "the opposite of a white cube gallery." Defined in part by the house's distinctive modernist architecture, La Loge's program extends beyond exhibitions to also include artist collaborations and theoretical explorations specific to the fields of visual arts, design and architecture. Recent projects have included a four-part series of design and architecture discussions hosted by UP, a local fanzine, who also transformed La Loge's exhibition space into a bar.

Middlemarch was founded in 2011 by Virginie Devillez, former curator at the Royal Museum of Fine Arts of Belgium and currently the director of Daniel Templon Gallery in Brussels, and artist Jean-Baptiste Bernadet. When Virginie couldn't find a space for a new contemporary art venue, she decided to use her own living room and dining room. After their first exhibition in October 2011 was a success, they decided to stick to the concept: "When an exhibition is hosted in someone's home people feel more comfortable and less intimidated," says Jean-Baptiste. Spotlighting local, emerging artists and side-projects is key to their vision, and they're careful to cultivate an open and diverse approach to programming which allows for everything from solo or group exhibitions to book launches and screenings.

MIDPOINT
189 Rue de Flandre Vlaamsesteenweg (1000)

NICC
1 Rue Lambert Crickx Straat (1070)
nicc.be

Ever since opening Midpoint in 2001, its founders have been inviting artists to create pieces that enhance the interior of this kitsch Rue de Flandre/Vlaamsesteenweg bar. "The social aspect of the project is very important to us," explains co-founder Alberto Garcia Del Castillo, who also is one of the directors at Komplot. For each new artwork there's a vernissage, and the party is part of the concept. Guest artists are encouraged not only to make an art piece but also to invite DJs. As the works are permanently integrated into the bar's interior and not marked, people who visit the bar don't even know they're looking at art. The project allows the artists to let their imagination run free, often to humorous effect.

Founded in 1998, the New International Cultural Centre (NICC) is an artist-run organisation that aims to strengthen the voice of artists in contemporary society and to defend their interests. They've got an activist attitude that's reflected in an annual programme that's packed with exhibitions, lectures, debates and talks by artists on the pressing issues of the day. Invitees have previously included such luminaries as skateboarder-turned-photographer Ed Templeton and Japanese contemporary artist Norio Imai.

RECTANGLE
189 Rue Emile Féronstraat (1060)
rectangle.be

SIC
54 Avenue Van Volxemlaan (1190)
sicsic.be

Artists Cédric Alby, Jérémie Boyard, Pierre-Pol Lecouturier and Xavier Pauwels founded Rectangle, an 11-square-metre billboard mounted on the rooftop of a former printing workshop, in 2012. Somewhat of an unlikely exhibition space, the advertising-inspired initiative leans heavily on the power of visual imagery by selecting, then broadcasting, one image which is chosen by the four artists. Some images are borrowed while others are made especially for the billboard. The artworks are for sale but the artists are quick to emphasise that the main goal is non-commercial; they are re-purposing the strategies of advertising campaigns in an urban surrounding. "It's a kind of silent activism. It's not aggressive, which is probably why it hasn't been taken down yet."

Founded in 2005, SIC exists primarily as an editorial and curatorial platform. The programme includes exhibitions, talks, conferences, performances, concerts and artist meetings, and is well-known for its yearly publication. In 2013, SIC was one of the few non-profit art spaces to be invited to Art Brussels, a well-deserved recognition thanks to a year long high-quality programme that included artists from Ivo Provoost and Fiona Mackay to Olivier Foulon.

SOTOSO
167 Boulevard Lemonnierlaan (1000)
sotoso.org

ART ASSIST
1a Rue Julien Dulait (6001)
facebook.com/artassist.vzw

Hans-Christian Lotz and Peter Wächtler host exhibitions in their own apartment. Going by the name of Sotoso, the pair, who are both artists themselves, organise expos based purely on their personal preferences and Georgia Sagri, Manuel Gnam and Nicola Brunnhuber have all made it into their home. But don't let the homely approach fool you: instead of integrating the artworks into their interiors, they've completely emptied a white-walled room for each artist.

Art Assist was founded by Gert Robijns in a converted garage. A large bay window overlooks a vast exhibition space that is used to exhibit Robijns' own work and that of others, and there are no rules and no agenda: Robijns calls it his 'test space'. Recently featured exhibitions have included a joint show by photographer Dirk Braeckman and painter Rezi van Lankveld, and a solo expo by sculptor Paul Casaer.

CROXHAPOX
76 Lucas Munichstraat (9000)
croxhapox.org

Founded in 1990 by Hans van Heirseele and Guido De Bruyn, Ghent's Croxhapox is one of the oldest spaces for emerging art in Belgium. For 20 years it has demonstrated a knack for recognising future big shots (it was one of the first to exhibit celebrated Belgian painter Michael Borrëmans). The project is open to all kinds of contemporary art including music, poetry and film, with special emphasis on promoting upcoming and unknown artists. Croxhapox is perhaps best described as an experimental art house, and artistic director Laura Van wants you to know that they are "*not* a gallery."

KIOSK GALLERY
2 Louis Pasteurlaan (9000)
kioskgallery.be

Though KIOSK is closely affiliated with nearby KASK art school, its programme is totally independent. "We exhibit a mix of emerging and established artists who have international potential... but are not famous yet," explains director Wim Waelput. KIOSK takes its time with each artist to work on the exhibition concept, making sure that there's a dialogue with the space itself. The programme places special emphasis on modernism, craftsmanship and social and political awareness with four exhibitions a year.

THESE THINGS TAKE TIME
36 Nederkouter (9000)
thesethingstaketime.be

GHENT

CIAP
21 Armand Hertzstraat (3500)
ciap.be

HASSELT

This art space features the standard-issue white cube atmosphere and large and inviting street-facing display windows. It was opened in April 2012 by graphic designer and fine arts student Matthias Yzebaert. "I have a bit of a problem with institutions like galleries, schools and museums and wanted to build my own little playground, a free zone without rules where everything is possible," says Matthias. The goal of the shows at These things take time isn't to sell stuff, but rather to present artworks that go against the common logic of the art world.

The non-profit CIAP was founded by a collective in 1976 and in 2009 moved to its current location, a former factory in Hasselt, where it hosts multidisciplinary exhibitions and lectures. With the support of the city and the province of Limburg (and under the tutelage of new director Ann Vanderheyden, formerly of Z33) CIAP aims to promote contemporary art in all its forms, based on the belief that it's vital for democracy. The recent show Traction Avant featured nine contemporary artists whose works were responses to the planned closure of the Ford factory in Genk. Other recent notable artists include Karen Vermeren and Lieven Nollet.

Z33

33 Zuivelmarkt (3500)
z33.be

HASSELT

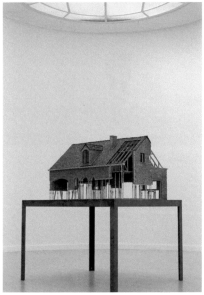

LA COMÈTE

213 Rue Vivegnis (4000)
e2n.be

LIÈGE

Z33, a famous name in Belgian contemporary art circles, is an experimental art and architecture museum in Hasselt. Located in a former nunnery that was taken over by the Province of Limburg in 1938, it's got a number of small spaces for site-specific works while larger exhibitions are hosted in Vleugel 58. Artists come from far and near, and Z33 doesn't have a permanent collection of its own but rather an ongoing programme of temporary exhibitions. There are three large and three smaller exhibition projects per year (Larry Bell, Mark Dion, Olafur Eliasson and Barry McGee...), often with a social theme, and apart from art expos the museum is famous for film and projections, and plays host to regional cultural happenings (as well as Manifesta 9 in 2012).

La Comète is an offshoot of Espace 251 Nord and is located at number 213 on the same street. It used to be a cinema, then a bicycle factory, and now it's a space devoted to artists (as opposed to a gallery) that offers creative residencies and production support to allow artists to bring their work face to face with the public. The aim is also to enhance and preserve the architectural heritage of the site itself, and the range of activities includes projections, performances, concerts, conferences, seminars and festivals.

ESPACE 251 NORD
251 Rue Vivegnis (4000)
e2n.be

LIÈGE

SPACE COLLECTION
116 En Féronstrée (4000)
space-collection.org

LIÈGE

Espace 251 Nord was founded in 1983 in Liège's old industrial district by a group of artists, headed by Laurent Jacob. With a massive 500 square metres dedicated to exhibitions, the mission is to enhance the visibility of Walloon and Brussels artists. "We have an original programme thanks to long-term relationships with artists and partners in northern Europe," says Laurent, whose collaborations have brought Espace 251 Nord to Rome, Venice, Florence, Lisbon, Paris and Lille. A large outer paved area hosts open-air exhibitions, concerts, festivals and carnivals and recent exhibitions have included Michael Dans and Christophe Terlinden.

Space Collection, founded in 2002 by the sculptor Alain De Clerck, is a mobile art collection that does the rounds of various spaces in Liège (Liège-Musée des Beaux-Arts, Liège SMartBe, Maastricht-SPACE and Liège-Courthouse). "It's a collection for the people, by the people," says De Clerck, whose aim is to provide financial support for young creatives in the city while making their art accessible to all. The collection is constantly expanding, and currently counts 60 pieces made up of all genres, materials and techniques, with works from artists such as Nina Berman, Eric Deprez and Charlotte Beaudry.

BRUSSELS PHILHARMONIC PRESENTS

2014·15

STARS

Michel Tabachnik
Ivo Pogorelich
Hervé Niquet
Daniel Hope
Stéphane Denève
Lars Vogt
Enrique Mazzolla
everin von Eckardstein

FILM

Das Cabinet des
Dr. Caligari
Der letzte Mann
West Side Story
Maudite soit la guerre

ON TOUR

London
Paris
Vienna
Edinburgh
Salzburg
Brussels

brussels
philharmonic

WWW.BRUSSELSPHILHARMONIC.BE

ssels Philharmonic is een instelling van de Vlaamse Gemeenschap · Eugène Flageyplein 18, B-1050 Brussel · +32 2 627 11 60 · info@brusselsphilharmonic.be

Pietro Celestina

35, was born in the Dutch Antilles. He moved to Antwerp where he co-founded Atelier Solarshop with fashion designer Jan-Jan van Essche.

on Antwerp's 2060 district

You know the Disney attraction, It's a Small World? Well that's 2060, the area around DAMEBRUGGESTRAAT. It's full of Moroccan and Chinese shops, African hairdressers and Pakistani suit shops, and it's a big inspiration for us. Lots of young artists are moving to the area, which is always how things go. We're near the DESIGN CENTER which is a sort of business complex for young creatives. It's good for the neighbourhood but it's hard to know if these young creative types will stay. Zuid used to be like this but lost its charm really fast and became a yuppie area as soon as all the working class people sold up and moved out. I don't leave the neighbourhood very much, I get my groceries on HANDELSTRAAT which is full of the kind of Moroccan and Turkish shops that are open all the time, weekends, Sundays whatever. They're very hard-working and they understand service, something modern culture has lost. MERSIN is a family-run grocery shop run by three young Turkish hipsters who are following in the steps of their grandfather. They're very friendly, and we talk about everything. I like going there; it's nostalgia but it's also about supporting each other's businesses. Most people around here live in small apartments with no gardens and one of the best developments in Antwerp over the past 20 years is a huge park called PARK SPOOR NOORD. It's a real success story. So many kinds of people sit together on the grass, there's a bar from April to September and fountains and a playground. It brings a lot of life to the area. The park connects 2060 to EILANDJE, which is a very modernised harbour full of yachts and lofts. It used to be abandoned warehouses, but now Dries Van Noten's HQ is there, as well as the recently-opened MAS museum. It's quite posh. On this side, the neighbourhood has some very negative connotations. It used to be a middle class area and the street where our shop is used to be full of fur shops. Some people who have watched the change from chic to ghetto are quite sad, and most of them left because they couldn't handle it. There's a café called VOGELENZANG, a very 'marginal' café, where every morning the locals go to sit and drink and stare out the window, the kind of people who've seen the transformation and they go there to complain to each other about it. But there's a project called NOORD FEESJES, an organisation that arranges parties in off-the-beaten-track venues that nobody would normally go to, like in Moroccan discos or Polish cafés, or in one of these typical Flemish working class bars. Very cool DJs come and the regulars are invited too. It's a way to connect people. This Vogelenzang was the location for one of the parties, and it got people mixing. It's a modern concept and it lifts a little bit of the tragic connotations. This neighbourhood has great potential: it used to be something, and it can be again. It's exciting to see what identity will emerge.

DESIGN CENTER
26 Lange
Winkelhaakstraat (2060)

MERSIN
38 Sint-Jansplein (2060)

PARC SPOOR NOORD
(2060)

→
VOGELENZANG
116 Lange
Beeldekensstraat (2060)

Dirk Braeckman

55, is a photographer and artist.
He was born in Eeklo but has spent most of his life in Ghent.

on Ghent Zuid

In my time, ZUID was another world. It used to be the film quarter
so there were lots of little cinemas, and the big one, CARTOONS,
which is still there. My earliest memories are of going with my parents
- and later, with friends - to watch films. That was the early '60s. But
then they dynamited the whole area and built the awful SHOPPING
CENTER ZUID. I'm still surprised after 25 years how awful this
building is. It's right at the entrance of Ghent where everyone arrives
by car from Brussels. The shame. Before they destroyed the area, it
was full of bars, discos, a boxing ring... I was living about 100 metres
away when they dynamited it. I was about 27 and I had a gallery with
CARL DE KEYZER in Brabantdam called XYZ. We called it that
because it was next door to a porn cinema – still there, 70 years later –
called ABC. We were good friends with the owner and we used to go
in and chat and have coffee and watch porn films. It was very bizarre.
It's Ghent's ROSSEBUURT, and we often worked with the skin clubs,
taking pictures of the girls. Anyway, there I was asleep and suddenly
I felt an explosion. I looked out my window and I saw them dynamiting
the whole area. So I took my camera – still in my pyjamas - and I started
taking pictures. I never did anything with them, though I have used
some of the negatives for other images. Since that day, the physiognomy
of Ghent has changed. The whole area was old and dilapidated and so
it's better now, I suppose, but I miss these bars and the old cinemas.
I miss the atmosphere. All the great clubs were in KUIPERSKAAI.
Back in the day it was the 55 CLUB, where Luc Tuymans was doorman
at one point. I remember giving him five Belgian francs. But the clubbing
days are long gone. These days Ghent clubbing is spread out, though
maybe you could say the new area is SINT-JACOBS. One thing that
has survived is the old socialist meeting place, the VOORUIT, which
was going to be demolished in the '80s until a bunch of artists protested
(and me and Carl made a film about it) and saved it. In the end, I closed
the gallery and I moved out of Zuid because I had a daughter and
I didn't want her growing up there. It's a bizarre place for children. I still
sometimes go though, because there are a couple of restaurants and
bars that I like, like the one across the street from the old gallery called
EL NEGOCITO. They haven't changed a thing in all these years. Yes,
I'm very nostalgic, but I also look to the future. It just hurts to see a
beautiful thing destroyed. You see it everywhere, especially in Brussels
and Antwerp. The only city that's safe is Bruges. Now Ghent is getting
better; they're going to change the façade of the shopping centre, and
they're tearing down Rabot Towers. I remember seeing them being
built when I was a kid. They were the biggest buildings that I had ever
seen and I was impressed, but they're actually really awful. The new
STADSHAL, designed by Robbrecht en Daem, is an example of a nice,
functional and integrated design, though people still protested against
it. But those people are stuck in the past. You see? It's not all about
nostalgia with me.

ABC
106 Brabantdam (9000)

EL NEGOCITO
121 Brabantdam (9000)

SHOPPING CENTRE ZUID
Woodrow Wilsonplein
(9000)

→
STADSHAL
Poeljemarkt (9000)

VOORUIT
23 Sint-
Pietersnieuwstraat
(9000)

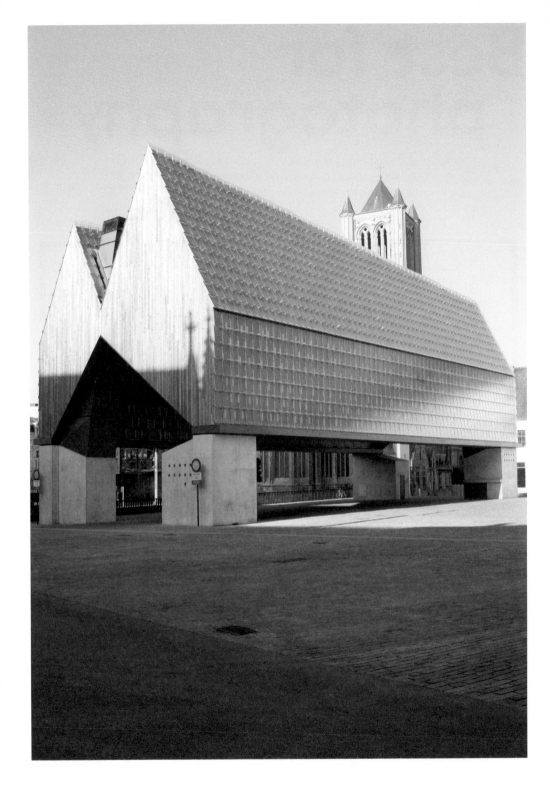

Best for photography

FIFTY ONE
FINE ART PHOTOGRAPHY GALLERY
Fifty One - 20 Zirkstraat (2000)
Fifty One Too - 2 Hofstraat (2000)
gallery51.com

FOMU
47 Waalsekaai (2000)
fotomuseum.be

Fifty One Fine Art Photography was founded back in 2000 by Roger Szmulewicz, who started taking pictures himself at the age of 16 – and who also happened to be the face, back in the day, for Ulrich Lang New York's perfumes Anvers and Anvers 2. One of the earlier, purely photography galleries in Antwerp, Fifty One enjoys a firm presence on the international scene, thanks to its outpost in New York and its impressive roster of photographers, which counts Ike Ude, William Klein and Seydou Keita amongst many others. A ten-year anniversary exhibition in 2013 presented photographs of Serge Gainsbourg, shot by the likes of Helmut Newton and Ulf Andersen, while it also has just recently opened a second outpost, Fifty One Too.

Antwerp's photography museum – known to locals as FoMu – opened in 1965 with the exhibition "125 years of photography". In October 1986 it moved from its Sterckshof location to its current 1,400 square-metre space that houses a bookshop, a movie theatre, a large library and a publishing arm responsible for two yearly publications: Extra and .TIFF (the latter focusing on emerging Belgian talent). The institution's impressive private collection spans the entire history of photography – including works by Man Ray, Brassai, Henri Cartier-Bresson, Irving Penn, William Klein and Andreas Gursky – while it also plays host to an array of lectures, workshops and portfolio reviews.

INGRID DEUSS GALLERY
11 Provinciestraat (2018)
ingriddeuss.be

STIEGLITZ 19
2 Klapdorp (2000)
stieglitz19.be

Ingrid Deuss, a freelance art buyer and producer working mostly in advertising and fashion, founded her eponymous gallery in 2011, making it one of the newest arrivals on the Belgian photography circuit. The gallery has gone on to establish a solid reputation for itself, owing mainly to its knack for acting as a platform for young talent to meet established photographers and show their works in spaces abroad. Previous exhibitions have included Karel Fonteyne, Marcel van der Vlugt as well as Rankin, and she's also mounted an exhibition in New York of the works of Nicolas Karakatsanis.

Since its opening in 2008, Antwerp's Stieglitz 19 has quickly established itself as one of Belgium's leading voices for emerging photography, its roster of artists counting photographers such as Devin Yalkin, Francois Goffin and Lara Gasparotto. Founded by Dries Roelens, the gallery plays a fine balancing act of presenting red-hot Asian talent alongside just-as-hot homegrown talent, two of its most recent shows being one of controversial Chinese photographer Ren Hang and the other by child prodigy photographer Lara Gasparatto. With such piping-hot signings, the gallery is today considered *the* place to be on opening night.

STILLL GALLERY
12 Laar (2140)
stilll.be

ANTWERP

44 GALLERY
44 Genthof (8000)
44gallery.be

BRUGES

Stilll Gallery, an initiative of curator Thierry Vandenbussche and writer/actor Rudy Morren, began in 2006 as a nomadic curatorial platform that has since spearheaded numerous solo and group exhibitions in Belgium and abroad. The latest arrival on the Belgian photography landscape, the gallery's opening show in October 2013 featured the works of Belgian photographer Jan Kempenaers in its 100 square-metre space which encompasses two rooms and a tiny library. Thierry and Rudy's stated mission is to show photography that deals with aesthetic, social and political questions; photography combined with painting, sculpture and performance. The gallery recently showed Unrecounted, the newest works of 4478zine founder Erik van der Weijde depicting Belgian ice-skating rinks.

Photographer Luc Rabaey founded 44 Gallery three and a half years ago, bringing some much-needed fresh air to the smallish Bruges art scene. The intimate space opened in April 2010 with an exhibition by Karen Borghouts and has since hosted an average of 12 shows a year, both solo and group exhibitions. Rabaey pays particular attention to the Belgian scene, having exhibited the works of homegrown photographers Max Pinckers, Jef Claes and Maroeskja Lavigne.

BOTANIQUE

236 Rue Royale / Koningsstraat (1210)
botanique.be

BOX GALERIE

88 Rue du Mail Maliestraat (1050)
boxgalerie.be

Although its core *raison d'être* remains showcasing independent and alternative music, Botanique's other love is photography. With somewhat of a knack for putting on shows that have been known to draw in the crowds – its 2012 exhibition on photo booths, 'Behind the curtain', was a hit – its programme delights by combining astute curatorial choices with a fresh approach to scenography. One of the unexpectedly nicer spaces to enjoy quality photography in Brussels, the vintage black and white photo booth right at the gallery's entrance is reason enough to drop in.

Brussels' Box Galerie came about in 2004 as the brainchild of Stefan De Jaeger, former adviser to photography collectors, and Alain D'Hooghe, photography historian, academic and founder of Cliché magazine. The gallery counts big shot Magnum photographer Harry Gruyaert and Sarah Moon on its roster whilst its inauguration exhibition featured Spanish photographer Toni Catany. Today counting two outposts, one located in the 100 square-metre space of an Ixelles / Elsene backyard and the other more of a 'corner' at the back of Filigranes book shop on Avenue Louis Lepoutrelaan, the gallery sits at the upper echelons of the collecting community in Brussels, most of its artists already being well-established.

BOZAR

23 Rue Ravensteinstraat (1000)
bozar.be

BRUSSELS

CONTRETYPE

1 Avenue de la Jonction
/ Verbindingslaan (1060)
contretype.org

BRUSSELS

Brussels' celebrated Centre for Fine Arts, or BOZAR, was built by legendary Belgian architect Victor Horta. It first opened its doors in 1928 and hosted the first International Exhibition of Photography the year after. It has seven artistic departments – from music and cinema to dance and literature – and the medium of photography is included in the Bozar Expo branch, led by Christophe De Jaeger, an art historian specialising in photography and new media art. The institution regularly features exhibitions of major photographers, like Canadian Jeff Wall and Belgian Charif Benhelima, and it also organises the biannual international Summer of Photography, the next edition of which kicks off during the summer of 2014.

Undoubtedly one of the country's most established photography spaces, Contretype was founded in 1978 by Jean-Louis Godefroid. The first curator to bring Robert Mapplethorpe to Belgium, Godefroid was a driving force behind the acceptance of photography as a fine art in Belgium, due in no small part to his life-long commitment to the centre. A non-profit that plays an important role in the country's photographic landscape, Contretype is especially supportive of homegrown artists in the early years of their careers, giving them a place to further explore their practice through exhibitions, conferences, artist talks, residencies, small-scale editions and access to the centre's tight-knit committee of curators, researchers and photography experts.

FONDATION A STICHTING

304 Avenue Van Volxemlaan (1190)
fondationastichting.be

BRUSSELS

GALERIE PARIS-BEIJING

66 Rue Hôtel des Monnaies (1060)
galerieparisbeijing.com

BRUSSELS

Opened in October 2012 by Astrid Ullens de Schooten (who herself is the owner of an impressive private collection of photography works) and Jean-Paul Deridder, Fondation A Stichting is set in shoe manufacturer Bata's former factories in the upcoming Forest / Vorst neighbourhood. The area is home to contemporary art centre WIELS, the curator-run art space Komplot, cultural centre Brass, and now, to Brussels' first private photography museum. Boasting an exhibition space of 450 square metres, the foundation's mission is to "further the creation, knowledge and preservation of photographic images" through a programme of exhibitions, book projects and workshops for young people. Recent shows have included German legends Bernd and Hilla Becher and the American photographer Lewis Baltz.

With branches in both Paris and Beijing, French-born Romain Degoul and Flore Sassigneux inaugurated their Brussels outpost in October 2013 with an exhibition of contemporary Chinese photography. Demonstrating a clear penchant for Asian art, their pairing of East and West photographers gives the gallery a distinctive niche to play in. Located in the gorgeous Hotel Winssinger, built in 1897 by Victor Horta, the gallery consists of two rooms, one of which was designed by the famous architect, and one modern white cube. Photographers who've graced its walls include Martin Parr, Laurent Chéhère and Li Wei.

RECYCLART

25 Rue des Ursulines
/ Ursulinenstraat (1000)
recyclart.be

BRUSSELS

MUSÉE DE LA PHOTOGRAPHIE

11 Avenue Paul Pastur (6032)
museephoto.be

CHARLEROI

Founded as a non-profit in 1997, Recyclart is located below the former train station of Bruxelles-Chapelle / Brussels-Kapellekerk. A multidisciplinary art centre whose photography programme is led by photographer Vincen Beeckman, one of the space's key strengths is promoting social cohesion by involving the locals in unorthodox photography projects such as, for example, a photo booth that travels through the neighbourhood capturing locals. With a determined focus on the talent coming out of the country's art schools, Recyclart is often the first to exhibit names you'll hear of in a few years time.

Located in a former monastery and founded in 1987, Charleroi's photography museum has become Europe's biggest – after it was renovated and enlarged to a size of more than 2,200 square meters in 2008. Its collection boasts more than 80,000 photographs, two million negatives, and documents charting all phases of photographic history, with an extensive library of about 13,000 books. Besides exhibitions, it also hosts workshops, film projections, talks and conferences. Under the tutelage of ambitious current director Xavier Canonne, the museum organises four major shows a year, with White Noise by Michel Mazzoni being one of its most recent and most successful.

GALERIE JACQUES CERAMI

346 Route de Philippeville (6010)
galeriecerami.be

COUILLET

LA GALERIE SATELLITE

20 Rue du Mouton Blanc (4000)
galeriesatellite.wordpress.com

LIÈGE

In 2001, Jacques Cerami founded an intimate gallery in a small town near Charleroi, opening with an exhibition of the works of painter Stéphane Vee. But being a multi-disciplinary art space, it was soon followed by a photography show by Véronique Ellena. "Photography asks more questions and tells more stories than other art forms," says Jacques, who admits that it's not always easy flying the photography flag in such a small rural town. "It's much easier to show photography in Brussels or Antwerp than here," he explains. The gallery represents photographers such as German Mirjam Siefert and Belgian Philippe Herbet, and its latest exhibition featured the works of Brussels-based artists Michel Couturier.

La Galerie Satellite was founded in November 2011 as part of the plastic arts department of Liège's Cultural Centre, Les Chiroux, in collaboration with non-profit project Les Grignoux. Dedicated to promoting contemporary photography, the centre's programme is overseen by Anne-Françoise Lesuisse, who pays close attention to the works of Brussels and Walloon artists. Case in point, previous exhibitions have included the works of photographers David Widart and Sarah Van Marcke, both of whom have emerged from the local photography scene over the last few years.

Fiona Mackay
Sisters

16.05 — 21.06.14

BELGIUM,
STEPHAN VANFLETEREN
(Lannoo, 2007)

Having been a photographer for Belgian
newspaper De Morgen from 1993 to 2009,
Vanfleteren benefits from an innate
understanding of the country's many different
facets. Best at capturing Belgium's everyday
people with his customary black and white,
grainy tones, Vanfleteren's book reveals the
honest and endearing truths of a country
hard at work.

DIRK BRAECKMAN,
DIRK BRAECKMAN
(Roma Publications, 2011)

The first comprehensive anthology of the
celebrated Ghent-based photographer's work,
Dirk Braeckman's book, at over 380 pages,
is a monumental testament to the artist's
oeuvre over the years. Published by Antwerp's
Roma Publications, it provides a fascinating
insight into one of the most deserving artists
of the last two decades, perfectly capturing
Braeckman's singular vision through a
combination of both existing and never-before-
seen prints.

MADE IN BELGIUM,
HARRY GRUYAERT
(Delpire, 2000)

A stark and frank portrayal that sometimes
borders on the grotesque, 'Made in Belgium'
epitomises the contrasting tones of the
country's many ordinary locals and their
often banal narratives. From city to seaside,
Gruyaert, a member of Magnum Photos,
captures both the beauty and the ugliness of a
nation steeped in surrealism with the distance
of an artist whose relationship to his country
is one of love and hate.

Iconic Belgian photography books

Best for
art books

COPYRIGHT ANTWERP
28a Nationalestraat 28a (2000)
copyrightbookshop.be

FOTOMUSEUM SHOP
47 Waalsekaai 47 (2000)
fotomuseum.be

Antwerp's spacious Copyright bookshop, with its swanky black marble interior, covers everything from architecture and design to fashion, and offers a very large selection of popular and specialist art books. Located within MoMu, the city's fashion museum, its featured publishers include Phaidon, Thames & Hudson, Mer, Lannoo and Roma Publications. It also has a nice selection of magazines such as Purple Fashion and A Magazine.

The shop connected to Antwerp's renowned FoMu opened in 2004 and sells a mixture of standard must-have art books, rare editions, exhibition catalogues and art publications. Come here to stock up on new and old titles by Belgian photographers like Jacques Sonck, Filip Claus, Filip Tas, Arno Roncada and Charlotte Lybeer, get your hands on a copy of the museum's own Extra and .TIFF magazines (the latter on emerging Belgian photography) or choose a museum souvenir from a handful of photography gadgets.

MASSHOP
1 Hanzestedenplaats (2000)
masshop.be

MUHKA SHOP
32 Leuvenstraat 32 (2000)
muhka.be

ANTWERP

The shop attached to the spectacularly-designed MAS museum is located in one of the pavilions, and features great big looming windows and an amazing view. It sells art books but also decorative items, publications for children and postcards. There's a focus on books connected to the history of the city, the museum architecture and collections (make sure to check out the book "The Making of the Mas") as well as special sections dedicated to Antwerp and Belgium.

The smallish bookshop attached to Antwerp's Museum of Contemporary Art, also known as MuKHA, has been around since 1993 and focuses on Belgian contemporary artists and architects. All of the books on sale here are related in one way or another to the museum, and the selection includes publications about such local luminaries as Guillaume Bijl, Panamarenko and Luc Tuymans.

CIVA BOOKS

55 Rue de L'Ermitage / Kluisstraat (1050)

COOK & BOOK

1 Place du Temps Libre
/ Vrijetijdsplein (1200)
cookandbook.be

Part of CIVA since its foundation in 1999, the bookshop connected to Brussels' International Centre for Urbanism, Architecture and Landscape is a paradise for all architecture aficionados. Small-sized but well-stocked, CIVA Books offers everything from architecture magazines such as The Japan Architect, MONU and CEBRA to books on designing schools, eco-architecture, gardening and urban planning. Classic monographs of star architects such as Le Corbusier or Gropius are available too, as well as all publications by CIVA's own publishing house, which wants to encourage research and debate about the relationship between human beings and their environment.

When Cook & Book opened in 2006 it was the talk of the town thanks to its novel concept: a bookshop with a restaurant attached, where you can sit, eat, read and try before you buy. There are nine different sections, each one decorated in a different and imaginative style (depending on the section – travel is decked out with an Airstream) and the clientele is very international. They have a very contemporary-looking and elaborately-stocked art book selection that always features some nice surprises for collectors with some beautiful special editions. Its magazine section stacks all types of contemporary titles on everything from graphic design and architecture to photography and interior design and it even has a few record crates where you might just find something to your liking.

FILIGRANES
39-40 Art Loi Kunstlaan (1040)
filigranes.be

LIBRAIRIE SAINT-HUBERT
2 Galerie du Roi / Koningsgalerij (1000)

Filigranes is one of Brussels' biggest generalists but the shop still manages to keep a cosy vibe (for those who prefer their bookshops on the more intimate side, there are smaller offshoots in the upmarket Uccle/Ukkel and Brugmann areas). The selection is enormous; the fine arts section is particularly extensive, as is the pick of magazines. It's mostly French, but there are sizeable other language sections, too (English in the basement). Despite its sprawling size, its comfy reading nooks and a café with a selection of coffee and cakes make it a tempting retreat for a sit-down and a chill-out.

Like Tropismes, Librairie Saint-Hubert is located in the art nouveau covered galleries near the Grand Place/Grote Markt (this particular spot was a pharmacy in the 19th century). Now, it's full of visual arts titles with a particular focus on photography. You can get your hands on publications by big shots like Dennis Hopper but also emerging local stars. The shop, whose beautiful wooden shelves and dominant chandeliers make for a very special atmosphere, also hosts photography exhibitions from time to time.

MONTANA SHOP & GALLERY
19 Rue de la Madeleinestraat (1000)
montanashop.be

PEINTURE FRAÎCHE
10 Rue du Tabellion Notarisstraat (1050)
peinture-fraiche.be

Opened in 2006 by former graffiti artist Nico, Montana Shop & Gallery is pretty much the reference for all things graffiti in Belgium. The official outpost to the legendary Spanish spray-paint of the same name, the shop stocks a considerable amount of specialist literature on graffiti culture, from publications on contemporary street art to visual biographies on the scene's legends. Somewhat of a meeting point for the city's relentless writer scene, the shop has just extended its space in order to be able to host more exhibitions with a special focus on urban themes.

Located in the heart of the upmarket Place du Chatelain / Kasteleinsplein area, Peinture Fraiche is an art, architecture, photography and design bookshop that has been around for more than 20 years. Now under new ownership and newly refurbished to afford it more space, its shelves feature a particularly hefty number of architecture and graphic design titles. Open from Wednesday to Saturday, the shop has a penchant for books on Japan, too – it's the owner-couple's second passion – whilst the magazine section stocks everything from Mousse to Elephant magazine. Add classical music and a no cell phone policy and you've got one of the city's most serene spaces to enjoy a good browse.

TASCHEN STORE
18 Rue Lebeaustraat (1000)
taschen.com

THÉOPHILE'S PAPERS
292 Chaussée D'Alsemberg
/ Alsembergsesteenweg (1190)
theophilespapers.tumblr.com

Housed in a corner house that sits right at the edges of Place du Grand Sablon / Grote Zavel, Taschen's Brussels flagship store is a dramatic display of the publishing house's grand vision of books. The shop exclusively sells Taschen editions, and it also has a gallery out back for one-off exhibitions and sales of tarnished and display copies.

Théophile's Papers was launched by French book fiend Théophile Calot and designer Valérian Goalec in March 2011, first setting up shop at Abilene Gallery then settling for his own space in December 2013. An itinerant, pop-up imprint that also includes a small corner in Paris' Préface Gallery, it exists as a platform for independent publishing houses, fanzines, journals and magazines which focus primarily on art, photography, typography and illustration. It's a very personal selection and the project is justly celebrated for its fresh scenography, which changes from place to place.

TIPI BOOKSHOP
186 Rue Hôtel des Monnaies
/ Munthofstraat (1060)
tipi-bookshop.be

TROPISMES
11 Galerie des Princes
/ Prinsengalerij (1000)
tropismes.com

Photography bookshop Tipi, opened in May 2013 by Italian-born Andrea Copetti, is located in a lovely little space in Saint-Gilles / Sint-Gillis with mosaic floors and beautiful wooden shelves from floor to ceiling. Copetti, a photographer himself, offers a fresh, offbeat selection of photography zines and self-published books, always on the lookout for new printing techniques and innovative ideas. Reflecting the store's goal to support and encourage artistic creation, Tipi refuses to deal with distributors and features quite a lot of titles from local artists such as Oliver Cornil and Vincent Delbrouck.

Tropismes is a generalist French-language bookshop located at the centre of Brussels in one of the gilded Galeries Royales Saint-Hubert/Koninklijke Sint-Hubertusgalerijen. It's an impressive space with a beautiful interior dripping with golden ornaments and mirrors spread over three levels, with the art department in the basement and a magazine rack lining the staircase. It offers a very nice selection of fine art books in every category from architecture to photography, and focuses more on content than stylish, attention-grabbing packaging.

WIELS BOOKSHOP
354 Avenue Van Volxemlaan (1190)
wiels.org

COPYRIGHT GHENT
8 Jakobijnenstraat (9000)
copyrightbookshop.be

Past the café and up the stairs to the left, right beside the reception, WIELS' bookshop sits on an open-plan set up that consists of three display units overflowing with all types of artist editions and contemporary art publications. An outpost of Berlin's celebrated Motto, the bookshop was opened in 2011 by Wim Clauwaert who carries everything from art publications and exhibition catalogues to obscure little fanzines and hard-to-find photography books. Having firmly established itself at the centre of the local publishing scene, the shop also runs the Pa/Per View art book fair, WIELS' artist edition festival that takes place every year in March.

Hilde Peleman had just graduated from her studies in art history when she opened Copyright Bookshop in Ghent (the first of the franchise), back in 1983. The bookshop specialises in art and architecture, focusing on contemporary artists and smaller publishers from Ghent, though you'll also find the more popular books too (Gestalten, Hatje Cantz, Poligrafa...). It's the perfect place for art lovers and is particularly popular among students from the nearby Sint-Lucas art school.

SMAK
Citadelpark (9000)
smak.be

M-SHOP
28 Leopold Vanderkelenstraat (3000)
mleuven.be

GHENT

LEUVEN

The bookshop attached to Ghent's famous SMAK. contemporary art museum features a wide range of must-have art books as well as exhibition catalogues and a good selection of magazines and fanzines. The under-30s can also buy a "Friends of SMAK" subscription here, which will get you good deals on limited edition signed and numbered prints. The visual experience is all important too, with all books displayed by their front cover.

M-Shop, attached to the Leuven Museum, mainly features books linked in one way or another to the museum's current exhibitions. Apart from in-house publications, high-quality art books and original children's books, there's also a nice selection of gifts. The bookshop's contents get updated every three months, just like the expos. There's a nice view and a cozy reading corner and lectures are organised frequently.

Inside
R.S.C.
Anderlecht

Depending on who you ask, the Constant
Vanden Stock stadium holds a special place
in the country's collective consciousness.
Home to the Royal Sporting Club Anderlecht,
or "Les Mauves' as they are known to local
supporters because of their purple shirts, the
stadium was built in 1917 and has a capacity of
28,000 spectators. Arguably one of the most
successful and popular Belgian football teams
ever (it counts 77 official fan clubs in Belgium
alone), the stadium currently has plans for an
extension, increasing its capacity to a reported
33,000 seats. With the country currently in the
midst of a football craze following the national
team's many successes, game nights at the
stadium are only sure to become livelier.

BUNKER PARADISE
(Stefan Liberski, 2005)

An unsettling, tense and dark portrayal of the cushioned lives of Brussels' moneyed elite, 'Bunker Paradise' captures the tragic collision of two worlds, one rich and yearning for more, the other modest and yearning for more too. With powerful performances by Jean-Paul Rouve and Bouli Lanners, the feature film goes from four-day house party marathon to suicidal early-morning hunting games. Despite its often-beautiful photography depicting the Brussels countryside's striking villas, the movie remains uncomfortable viewing for the realities it lays bare.

C'EST ARRIVÉ PRÈS DE CHEZ VOUS
(Rémy Belvaux, André Bonzel and Benoit Poelvoorde, 1992)

The film that introduced Belgium to the world, 'C'est arrivé près de chez vous' is a mockumentary which follows the exploits of a madman serial-killer rapist on a rampage. A dark comedy that goes from poems for pigeons to midnight chases in the forest, the film, which has since gained cult status, challenged what was then deemed acceptable. With one of Belgian actor Benoît Poelvoorde's most memorable performances, the movie delights with its typical Belgian prose, situations and characters.

DE HELAASHEID DER DINGEN
(Felix Van Groeningen, 2006)

The Belgium depicted in Felix Van Groeningen's film adaptation of Dimitri Verhulst's book (called 'La Merditude des Choses' in French) is bleak. The movie tells the story of Gunther Strobbe, who lives with his father, grandmother and three uncles in a cramped and destitute house in a small Flemish countryside village. Torn between the urge to escape his unruly elders' antics (drinking cheap beer and running after the local women) and remaining loyal to the Strobbe family name, his values are finally tested when a social worker forces Gunther to board at school. Drawing on authentic Flemish living and landscapes, the movie immerses the viewer in a dreary, depressing and deflated Belgium.

STRIP-TEASE
(Marco Lamensch and Jean Libon, 1985)

"I always say that if anthropologists want to study Belgium, viewing Strip-tease's 800-or-so episodes [would provide] an extremely accurate and uncut portrayal of the country and its people," says Jean Libon, co-creator of the cult TV series that first began airing on Belgium's French-speaking broadcaster RTBF in 1985. They went on to produce an episode a month until broadcasts ceased in 2002. "Our aim was to give authentic people a voice on television," and, with its first episode, 'L'Arche de Zoé', which tells the story of the cash-strapped father of ten who kills the neighbour's sheep in order to put food on the table, the tone was set right from the get-go. Essential episodes include 'Monseigneur au Vatican' (Belgium's official at the Vatican, 1991), 'Merci, Patron' (A Belgian retiree and his maid in Zaire, 1998) and 'Monsieur le Bourgemestre' (on Brussels' former mayor Hervé Brouhon, 1985).

THE SOUND OF BELGIUM
(Jozef Devillé, 2013)

Making a movie about Belgium's considerable contribution to electronic music was always going to be a challenging task. To most, new beat is where it begins. But dig a little deeper, and you'll find that Belgium's propensity for pre-recorded popular music goes back as far as the 1920s, with the invention of the Decap organ. And that's only one of the many interesting revelations of first-time director Jozef Devillé's ambitious feature-length, The Sound of Belgium. Drawing on interviews with DJs, producers, records collectors, label heads and other legends of the times, as well as on hours of painstakingly-researched archival footage, the movie touches upon the country's every musical phases, from popcorn and new beat to dance and house music, finally giving Belgium its due.

Iconic Belgian films

Best for arthouse cinema

CINEMA ZUID
14 Lakenstraat (2000)
cinemazuid.be

DE ROMA
286 Turnhoutsebaan (2140)
deroma.be

Cinema Zuid is a non-profit initiative of Antwerp's modern art museum, MuHKA, whose stated goal is to teach and to entertain by promoting a deeper understanding of film, video and television culture. It's a place to go for movies new and old, and not just classics or auteur cinema, but also popular genre films, documentaries, animation, experimental cinema, trash/cult... and visitors are also invited to participate in lectures, courses and workshops. Movie-going for the high-minded.

De Roma, located in Antwerp's Borgerhout district, has been around since 1928, making it one of Belgium's oldest cinemas. A beautiful and historic building, it used to be a concert venue and welcomed legends such as Lou Reed and James Brown. Closed in 1982, it reopened again in 2003 and now offers a vast and eclectic cultural programme not limited to cinema but also readings, concerts, theatre and dance performances. Arguably one of the most architecturally-stunning cinema houses in Belgium.

KLAPPEI
2 Klappeistraat (2060)
klappei.be

LUMIÈRE CINEMA
36 Sint-Jakobsstraat (8000)
lumierecinema.be

The beautiful-if-pokey building that houses De Klappei used to be a 19th century police station (the men's room is a former cell and still features the original bars) and was last renovated in 1916. There's a bar with movie posters on the walls and directors' chairs where you can enjoy a drink, and some nice art deco touches. The screening room itself is tiny, and they show classics and independent movies; everything from travelogues to super-violent feature-lengths. As there's only one room there's not much choice, and it's often empty. The plush red chairs are a pleasure. Make sure to say thanks on your way out because all the workers are volunteers.

Bruges' Cinema Lumière has been around for over a decade. It's located right in the city centre in a gorgeous old building where it screens independent movies and hosts the Cinema Novo Film Festival. It's attached to a publishing and distribution house which distributes a selection of Scandinavian crime series as well as European arthouse films like The Misfortunates. It's even produced a short film by Raoul Servais.

ACTOR'S STUDIO
16 Petite rue des Bouchers
/ Korte Beenhouwersstraat (1000)

CINEMATEK
9 Rue Baron Hortastraat (1000)
cinematek.be

Located just around the corner from the Grand Place / Grote Markt, the Actor's Studio, accessible through the lobby of the Floris Arlequin Hotel, is a lovely little nostalgia-inducing cinema with a small bar and two charming screening rooms. It shows a good mix of carefully-chosen Hollywood productions and lesser-known arthouse flicks and is a favourite with late-night moviegoers looking for something with a twist.

A Belgian institution founded in 1938, Cinematek is home to the Royal Belgian Film Archive and houses one of the richest film collections in the world. It's both a museum and working cinema that hosts five daily screenings of everything from the classics to amateur productions and documentaries in its two well-equipped screening rooms. It often dedicates entire monthly schedules to a certain director, genre or country and is appreciated by hard-nosed cinephiles for its high-browed and cerebral take on the fifth art. Films are screened in their original format and language (silent films are accompanied by piano music) and there's a modern exhibition hall where you can check out digitised versions of rare archive footage.

CINEMA FLAGEY
Place Sainte Croix
/ Heilig Kruisplein (1050)
flagey.be

CINEMA GALERIES
26 Galerie de la Reine
/ Koninginnegalerij (1000)
galeries.be

The popular art deco cultural centre located on Place Flagey / Flageyplein is an institution open to all artistic disciplines but for whom film holds a special place. Frequently featuring movie cycles such as the recent Alfred Hitchcock and James Stewart retrospectives, Cinema Flagey also participates in film festivals and regularly collaborates with other cultural institutions like Bozar and Cinematek. In the summer, there's even an open-air cinema beside the bustling concrete jungle that is Place Flagey.

Brussels' newest addition to the independent cinema scene, Cinema Galeries opened in 2012. Located in the former premises of the beloved Cinema Arenberg in the lovely Galerie de la Reine/Koninginnegalerij, its new directors have renovated the screening rooms and added an exhibition space, a bar and a shop. The programme focuses on films by contemporary directors and also special events for kids. It's open every single day, with movie screenings from 11 in the morning till midnight.

CINEMA NOVA
3 Rue D'Arenbergstraat (1000)
nova-cinema.org

STYX
72 Rue de l'Arbre Bénit
/ Gewijde Boomstraat (1050)
cinema-styx.wikeo.be

Cinema Nova is a non-profit staffed mostly by volunteers with a programme organised around monthly themes such as 'The Beat Generation' or 'The Berlin Wall'. Concentrating on quirky, independently-produced and unconventional films, it screens feature but also short, documentary and experimental films as well as productions that cannot find a distributor. Cinema Nova also puts on concerts, exhibitions and performances and it's even evolved into a small distribution and production house. More than a mere cinema, to many local flick fiends Nova is a way of life.

The down-homey independent cinema Styx opened its doors more than four decades ago. With only two rooms boasting all of 38 seats each, it's the smallest cinema in Brussels – and even at that, screenings almost never sell out, giving it a living-roomy feel. Located behind the Solvay building in a typical Ixelles/Elsene townhouse, it's a very cosy and intimate place whose programme focuses on high-quality repeats, arthouse productions, classics and independent releases.

VENDÔME

18 Chaussée de Wavre
/ Waversesteenweg (1050)
cinema-vendôme.be

ART CINEMA OFFOFF

237 Lange Violettestraat (9000)
offoff.be

Founded in 1952 by Henry Fol, the family-run Cinema Vendôme, nestled in the heart of the city's Matonge neighbourhood, has had quite a long history pushing their passion for the art of film on the Brussels populace. With a penchant for original, intimate and inventive films, it's got five projection rooms and an eclectic programme that tilts heavily towards the independent and foreign. The cinema also regularly participates in local and international film festivals, including the Millennium International Documentary Film Festival as well as the European Short Film Festival.

Art Cinema OFFoff is a non-profit screening and research platform for experimental film. Its programme is directed towards an audience that appreciates the more formal and esoteric aspects of the genre; it likes to screen avant-garde productions from rising stars, and pays close attention to the more obscure moments in cinema history. OFFoff also organises lectures that serve as a discussion forum for film-related topics.

KASK CINEMA
4 Godshuizenlaan (9000)
kaskcinema.be

SPHINX
3 Sint-Michielshelling (9000)
sphinx-cinema.be

GHENT

GHENT

The building that houses Sphinx was constructed in 1912 and is protected as a cultural heritage monument. While it's always been used to screen films, it's only been known as Sphinx since 1986 when it started screening a carefully-selected mixture of blockbusters and arthouse movies, with a special focus on international film festivals from Cannes to Toronto. It's also got special screening cycles and participates in film festivals.

KASK Cinema is an initiative of KASK, the city's art school, and mostly screens contemporary and undistributed films that test the boundaries of the medium, from pioneering and quirky productions to major milestones in movie history. The programme includes lectures, readings and debates, and every last Sunday morning of the month they even organise something for the little ones.

STUDIO SKOOP

63 Sint-Annaplein (9000)
studioskoop.be

Studio Skoop is Ghent's oldest working cinema and combines nostalgic old-school movie-pleasure with modern projection gear. Consisting of five small and intimate projection rooms nestled in a beautiful old building, it's been open since the '70s showing everything from Japanese classics from the '60s to new hand-picked internationally-acclaimed productions. There's also a nice bar with drinks, decked out with old film posters and photographs.

LES GRIGNOUX

CINEMA LE PARC
22 Rue Paul-Joseph Carpay (4020)
CINEMA CHURCHILL
20 Rue du Mouton Blanc (4000)
CINEMA SAUVENIÈRE
12 Place Xavier-Neujean (4000)
grignoux.be

Liège's cultural centre, Les Grignoux, includes three cinemas in three different locations: Parc, Churchill and Sauvenière. It's got a long history as a meeting point for the socially-conscious, and there are plans to open up a branch in Namur in 2015. Parc and Churchill are rather small-sized cinemas that concentrate mainly on arthouse movies, while Sauvenière, the newest, is housed in a bigger complex with a number of screening rooms and its own brasserie. These cinemas screen the odd blockbuster and sometimes host festivals.

THIS IS **ANTWERP**
ART // MUSIC // FASHION // LIFE

YOUR LOCAL GUIDE IN YOUR POCKET.

Download the THIS IS ANTWERP cityguide for iPhone and Android and discover the hidden secrets of young Antwerp.
You can find our magazine and monthly calendar all throughout the city.

follow us on
twitter.com/_thisisantwerp_
instagram.com/thisisantwerp

FREE APP!

ANDROID APP ON
Google play

Available on the
App Store

CITY OF ANTWERP

www.thisisantwerp.be

Kaat Debo

37, is from Antwerp and is the current director of MoMu.

on Antwerp's
2000 district

Before the eighties nothing really happened in this neighbourhood, and then Dries Van Noten came and opened MODEPALEIS. It was a big risk; it was the very first fashion store on NATIONAALESTRAAT, which at the time was just a really sad-looking grey street. So Dries wasn't just there in the beginning. He *was* the beginning. Soon after, the MODE MUSEUM opened and it brought new life to the neighbourhood. We're right next to the poor neighbourhood of Sint Andries, and when I talk about poor, I don't mean immigrants, I mean the original working class locals who've been here forever and SINT ANDRIESPLAATS is a nice little square where they drink strong beers in the afternoon. What do they think about fashion and Dries van Noten and all that? I think they find it kind of nice that the neighbourhood is appreciated again. What I don't know is how it affects rental prices. In 2001 Ann de Meulermeester designed an outfit for the statue of the VIRGIN MARY IN THE LOCAL SINT-ANDRIES CHURCH. It's a beautiful dress made out of feathers and she's still wearing it. Nationalstraat is really long and the further south you go, the more diverse it gets. It suddenly starts to get more commercial and you start to see lots and lots of five-euro shops. And lots and lots of hairdressers. Don't ask me why. I like the antique shops on nearby KLOOSTERSTRAAT, which has always been the place for brocante in Antwerp. I think it's important to preserve the past – we have to innovate but at the same time make sure to keep the diversity of what went before. One place I love is this very old glove store called HUIS A. BOON. Fifty years ago it was very normal to have accessory stores like that, to have tailors who measured your body and made something just for you. Now when you buy clothes, half the time people who sell them to you know nothing about the product and they don't care. There was a time when hats were an obligatory accessory, when you would never leave the house without one. That was until the entire youth revolution in the sixties when the attention was more on hair and we lost that accessory. And so we also lost all these shops. It's a pity, I think. Near Klossterstraat is the SINT-ANNATUNNEL, a pedestrian walkway that goes under the Scheld river. The architecture is amazing, you have to take this old escalator down into it, and a lot of artists and photographers seem to have found it and have been making their videos there. Once you get to the other side of the river there you can eat pancakes and waffles with the locals with a nice view of Antwerp's skyline and even a fake beach called SINT-ANNA STRAND, where some locals spend their annual holidays! It's really typical Antwerp.

HUIS A. BOON
2 Lombardenvest (2000)

MODEPALEIS
16 Nationaalstraat (2000)

MODE MUSEUM
28 Nationaalstraat (2000)

→
SINT-ANNATUNNEL
Sint-Jansvliet (2000)

THIS IS BELGIUM   74

Best
for city
views

PARKING 58
BRUSSELS

Once you get past the screeching, outdated elevator and get onto the tenth floor, Brussels' city centre is laid out at your feet. Known as the best free view in the city, with views on a clear sunny day stretching north to the Atomium and south to Forest / Vorst's Altitude 100 / Hoogte Honderd, the rooftop also plays host to parties such as Les Jardins Suspendus.

1 Rue de l'Evêque / Bisschopsstraat

MAS MUSEUM

Although the rooftop of Antwerp's MAS – an architectural tour de force by Neutelings Riedijk Architects – is open to the public all year round, the museum turns their highest floor into a night sky observatory every Thursday evening during the summer. The view of Antwerp from this high-end architectural jewel is amazing, and when clear, even the planets Venus and Saturn can be seen in all their glory.

1 Hanzestedenplaats
mas.be

M WITH A VIEW

Located high in the modest penthouse of
an old factory building, we get the whole
007 vibe the people behind Ghent-based
restaurant Coeur d'Artichaut have put into
their rooftop restaurant concept. With a
menu that changes only every few months,
you can bet your boots that whatever ends
up on your plate has been handled with
care and conscientiousness. You might
want to make a reservation though as
tables tend to go fast.

110 Gasmeterlaan
m-gent.be

J'AIME LA VIE
(SANDRA KIM, 1986)

Released as a 7" on French record label
Carrere, 'J'aime la vie,' sang by a then-
thirteen-year-old Sandra Kim, won Belgium
the Eurovision song contest in 1986.

BEATS OF LOVE
(NACHT UND NEBEL, 1983)

Epitomising Belgium's new wave resurgence
in the early '80s, Nacht und Nebel's much-
covered 'Beats of Love' went on to sell over
150,000 copies. The song was the first single
from the album of the same name, released
on prolific Belgian new beat producer Roland
Beelen's Antler Records.

QUI (M'A ENLEVÉ)..?
(BRUSSELS SOUND REVOLUTION, 1989)

A Belgian prime minister gets kidnapped by
the country's most infamous outlaw, Patrick
Haemers. At a press conference following
his release, his words are recorded by sound
engineer Paul Delnoy. The rights to the sound
snippets are sold on to producer Jacky Mauer,
who loops the conference's most memorable
moments, going on to make new beat history
with what is without a doubt one of the
weirdest tracks to grace mid-'80s dance floors.
Over 50,000 units were sold of the single,
released on defunct imprint Sound of Belgium.

Iconic Belgian records

Best for
records

CHELSEA RECORDS
10 Kloosterstraat (2000)

Only slightly larger than your average living room, this claustrophobic vinyl-only record shop is located at the end of Antwerp's tourist-heavy antiques street, Kloosterstraat. It's been open for more than 20 years. The records are well-classified and easy to find but stacked away in tiny boxes, making it a bit of a pain for digging. Come here for rock, reggae, house, soul, funk and disco. There's no computer in the shop and no online sales – everything hand-to-hand, nice and old-school – just the way owner Pascal likes it.

COFFEE & VINYL
45 Volkstraat (2000)
coffeeandvinyl.com

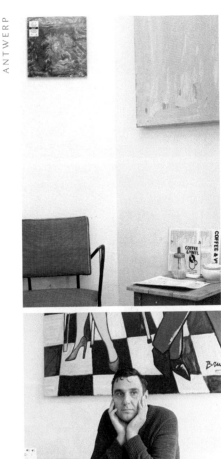

Lars Cosemans used to run a popular spot called Vinyl Records in the city centre but moved to Antwerp's Zuid neighbourhood to open this concept-heavy enterprise in 2011. It's perhaps the only place that combines a bar and café with a vinyl shop and art gallery. He buys and sells new and second-hand vinyls and second-hand-only CDs. The staff have a reputation for being none too pleasant, but the concept gets our vote. They've got a record of the week thing on Facebook and a turntable so you can try before you buy.

FAT KAT

51 Lange Koepoortstraat (2000)
fatkat.be

This place is run by a couple of really friendly people. Co-founder Staf de Vos says that he only looked up the meaning of the term 'fat cat' after he had already named the shop, and he insists he's a nice guy and not a money-grubbing arsehole. We are inclined to agree, as are the hordes of record lovers who flock regularly to his city-centre shop. It's been around 15 years, and the stock is 50/50 vinyl and CDs, both new and second-hand. The selection features the lot: from rock, '60s psychedelia, punk and hardcore to reggae, soul and funk.

TUNE UP

17 Melkmartkt (2000)
tuneuprecords.com

Located above IMS Melkmart (one of the city's finest international newssagents), the tastefully-decorated Tune up is adorned with musically inspired art, and has its own café. The owners, Carlo (a former DJ) and Michel, are really sweet guys who sometimes host live gigs. It's a bit of a hotspot for the steady stream of hardcore Antwerpenaar crate diggers (for some reason, record collectors in Antwerp are really that: hardcore) and he counts the guys of Deus, Zita Swoon and Suki Love among his loyal customers. The selection of goods is general and the prices are hardly bargain basement, but not too steep either.

WALLY'S GROOVE WORLD
126 Lange Nieuwstraat (2000)
wallysgrooveworld.com

72 RECORDS
72 Rue du Midi / Zuidstraat (1000)

This is Antwerp's answer to Doctor Vinyl, only better organised. The shop used to be located in the basement of USA Import, a legendary new beat label, and the guy behind the counter is Koenie, a DJ and famous fixture on Belgium's nightlife landscape. He started his mixing career in the '80s and was once resident DJ at Cafe D'Anvers. This is *the* place to go for second-hand electronic music records – not many record shops can say that – and Koenie is quite experienced (and also quite intense, if you don't mind us saying).

This tiny, vinyl-only, shop on Rue du Midi / Zuidstraat, Brussels' unofficial crate-digging main drag, was opened in September 2012 by a guy called Touki. Touki sells a bit of everything, though he has a particular penchant for punk and hardcore records, most of them second-hand. It's perhaps no accident that it's located just a hop, skip and jump from DNA Café.

ARLEQUIN

7 Rue du Chêne / Eickstraat (1000)
arlequin.net

CAROLINE MUSIC

101 Boulevard Anspachlaan (1000)
carolinemusic-bxl.be

Arlequin has two outlets: one in Saint-Gilles / Sint-Gillis (which replaced the old one in Ixelles / Elsene) and the other one 20 metres from the Manneken Pis. Perhaps the most organised record shop on the list – all artists get their own section – both Arlequins are far easier to navigate than their slipshod sisters. There's an emphasis on reggae although both outlets stock strong collections, with an especially good selection of well-priced new wave records. Don't expect too much assistance from the store's staff though, as they usually like to keep to themselves.

Brussels' de facto home to the alternative set, Caroline Music is the grand old dame of Brussels record stores, having first opened in Ixelles/Elsene back in 1972. After a decade in the city's Passage Honoré, it merged with fellow downtown record shop Goupil-o-Phone back in 2012 to set up a new outpost on Boulevard Anspachlaan, their current two-floor location. Your archetypical record store (think High Fidelity), this is the kind of place where you'll end up spending an hour talking to the guys behind the counter, coming out with a much bigger stack of records than you had originally planned for. The kind of store that sends you a text message when your order has arrived.

DOCTOR VINYL

1 Rue de la Grande Ile
/ Groot Eilandstraat (1000)
doctorvinylrecords.be

ELEKTROCUTION

37 Rue des Pierres / Steenstraat (1000)

Geert Sermon opened his iconic record store, a cramped space nestled in the heart of the city's Saint-Gery / Sint-Goriks district, back in 1997. One of the driving forces behind 2013's new beat documentary The Sound of Belgium (he compiled the box set that accompanied the already classic movie), Geert is a former DJ who mostly peddles dance and house records – all of them new releases. The kind of place where regulars get white labels, imports and exclusives set aside for them, the shop is the hangout for most local DJs (not that they buy anything). Fact is, ask any DJ worth his record collection and latest mix about Doctor Vinyl and chances are he'll have a story to tell. Belgian electronic music, and Brussels, would be nothing without this man and his legendary store.

Another punk and hardcore outlet (there's plenty of demand), Elektrocution is run by local headbanger hero Michel Kirby, one-time guitarist for Mental Disturbance and Deviate (the first band signed to legendary I Scream Records). He currently plays with the groups Length of Time, Goatcloaks and Arkangel, and his shop attracts a loyal fan base. Crates stock everything from electro goth, industrial and neo-folk to heavy and thrash metal, and customers here are well-known for being rather... special. Black everything, basically.

HORS-SERIE
67 Rue du Midi / Zuidstraat (1000)

JUKE BOX
165 Boulevard Anspachlaan (1000)
jukeboxshop.be

This is actually a bookshop with a decently-stocked first floor of second-hand vinyls, as well as a limited-print sheet music section. The space is big, the selection quite general, the CD collection not bad, and there's quite a good smattering of French pop and jazz. It's also well-known for being well-priced. They sometimes put on modest expos, particularly on the subject of jazz. Unfortunately (or fortunately) Hors-Serie is often overlooked; most would-be customers mistake it for a mere bookshop.

Juke Box fits the romantic, clichéd ideal of the typical, dusty old record shop – a small, messy room with records spilling from every corner. The oldest record shop in Brussels, Juke Box is run by a guy called Jean-Pierre who's about 65-ish, and who also runs the annual record fair in Galerie Ravenstein which takes place in June this year. This is a good place to find rare records if you're ready to fork out as Jean Pierre feels no compulsion to charge reasonable prices – the reputation his shop enjoys means clients just keep coming back.

MONSIEUR JEAN
9 Avenue Latérale / Zijlaan (1180)

RECORD COLLECTOR
26 Rue de la Bourse / Beursstraat (1000)
the-collector.be

This very interesting little record shop is far-out. Literally. Located in Vivier d'Oie / Diesdelle in the posh Brussels neighbourhood of Uccle / Ukkel, it's as far from the beaten record-hunting track as you can get. The owner is a character who looks a bit like eccentric Dutch poet Jules Deelder and whose shop has been open for a few years now. He also sells books, comics and vintage stereos as well as other hi-fi gear and there's a very decent jazz selection. It's a bit of a trek to get to, which makes the digging all the more rewarding.

Located on one of the many hectic side streets that hug the Bourse / Beurs, family-run Record Collector gets its fair share of passing tourist trade. It's a bit like Juke Box in that it fits the nostalgic image of an old-school record store – old, dusty and jumbled with records piled onto every available inch of floor space. Although the selection is rather general, from jazz to funk to pop, it's got an impressive back catalogue of records that's always sure to pull up the odd gem or two.

VEALS & GEEKS

8 Rue des Grands Carmes
/ Lievevrouwbroerstraat (1000)
vealsandgeeks.com

MUSIC MANIA

19 Sint-Pietersnieuwstraat (9000)
musicmaniarecords.be

Veals & Geeks, an old faithful on Brussels' vinyl freaks' route that opened in 2008, has a bunch a well-curated crates that tilt towards krautrock, prog rock and new wave. The store is staffed by very nice people (rare) and attracts a regular influx of curious tourists due to it being on the way to the Manneken Pis. The back-stock is just enormous, with lots of new records coming on a regular basis. The quintessential record store, Veals & Geeks also sells books, magazines, vintage types and all sorts of hard-to-find specialist memorabilia. What's more, it sits right opposite Lady Paname, the city's foremost purveyor of kinky wear.

Founded in 1969, Music Mania is the reference that all Belgian record stores aspire to and is often cited as the country's quintessential record store (think London's Rough Trade). It's got a fine mix of a bit of everything: new indie releases, old house records, cosmic Italian disco, a bit of a Ballaeric influence as well as the odd hip hop classic. It's well-laid-out, well-run, and the collection gets refreshed often by a dream team of well-known collectors that includes DJ Lorin, one of the most reputed disco collectors in Belgium, and Adriaan Denoorme, the guy behind Borat76, one of the best Belgian Discogs stores around. One for the '90s history vaults: Music Mania used to have a Brussels outpost, with none other than Giles Peterson protégé and Stones Throw affiliate Lefto behind the counter.

MUSIC ZOMBI
21a Keizer Karelstraat (9000)
musiczombi.com

VYNILLA
38 Sint-Kwintensberg (9000)
vynilla.be

Ghent's Music Zombi is stocked with mainly electro records, but it's got some other stuff too. It's mostly new releases but you'll also come across some pre-loveds. Yves 'Biens' Boone, of now-defunct Music Man label fame and former resident at Culture Club, opened it in 2012. He's your typical ex-DJ who might comes across as a bit intense at first (he really likes to talk) but overall is lovely. A good shop with a truly decent selection, it's the kind of store that just might stock that record you never thought you'd lay your hands on.

Vynilla has been based in Ghent since 1981. The shop and the website are run by a very knowledgable guy called Bob, and it's a good place for buying and selling second-hand vinyl and CDs. Their website offers only a taste of his actual stock, which is really quite substantial. There are lots of collectables and the selection is quite general, with special emphasis on Belgian vinyl: from rock to new wave to industrial electronic, minimal, experimental, black, world, jazz...

VINYL KITCHEN
160 Lange Violettestraat (9000)
vinylkitchen.be

WOOL E SHOP
17 Emiel Lossystraat (9040)
wool-e-shop.be

This record shop on Lange Violettestraat is a bit out of the city centre. The stock is general and not too remarkable and the prices are fair. The records are a mix of everything; soul, funk, disco, punk, metal, new wave, classical, world music, hip hop, house, reggae, blues and soundtracks... and the same goes for the clientele. New records come in on Wednesdays and they can be found in the crates at the counter, or you can check them out on Facebook. There are even a few chairs and turntables for your chilling and listening pleasure.

This is a firm favourite among hardcore collector freaks. It's run by a friendly guy called Dimitri, a true child of the '80s who specialises in all things wave: new wave, dark wave, minimal wave, cold wave... though there's more to Wool E than that. The shop is actually in the front room of a house, and it's pretty tiny and full. They also sell records at gigs and festivals both at home and abroad, so be sure to check the schedule because the shop is closed when they're out and about flogging their wares.

CARNABY RECORDS
10 Place Saint-Pholien (4020)

LIÈGE

THE VINYL TOUCH
1 Haverwerf (2800)
thevinyltouch.be

MECHELEN

Liège's only record shop worth mentioning, Carnaby Records in Outremeuse is another establishment that fits the romantic ideal of ye olde record shop (a bit dirty, dark and run-down looking). It's got an okay selection of vinyls and CDs covering lots of '70s and '80s rock, but also a bit of techno and everything in between. There are some nice rarities and lots of bootlegs. The two guys behind the counter are approachable experts, and the prices are not bad either.

This shiny new record shop in Mechelen's centre is a kind of Veals & Geeks but for locals. Opened in 2012, it used to be housed in a smaller location but is now in a much bigger space in a brand new building next to the city's cultural centre. Founder Emiel Van Geebergen is a longtime jazz, blues and soul record collector and his collection grew so big that the only option was to open a shop. His crew is made up of him, his sons and his wife and he's got a decent stockpile of about 30,000 records with plenty of jazz, soul pop, '60s to '90s rock, both new and second-hand. The shop also sells stamps for serious philatelists.

VEALS & GEEKS
9 Rue des Carmes (5000)
vealsandgeeks.com

NAMUR

K RECORDS
5 Waversesteenweg (2580)
k-records.be

PUTTE

The sister establishment to the Brussels shop of the same name, this Namur outpost was opened by owner Stanislas because he simply had too much stock, but also because he knew the city well, having previously worked for Music Emporium for 20 years, and knew there was a need. "Namur has no Media Markt, no FNAC, no competition," he says. The shop's spirit is the same although the space is smaller. His crates mostly stock '60s and '70s rock, but he's also got a good range of progressive and psychedelic rock as well as rap. New and second-hand stock, and it's vinyl only.

K Records, which does most of its trade online thanks to its remote location in the little lost Flemish town of Putte, is filled with electronica: house-trance, minimal, electro, Goa, club, groove and experimental... Since opening in 1998, the physical shop has been located in a converted garage owned by local boy Kurt De Preter (the older generation might remember former DJ Kurt K form Lier's Club Illusion or his residency at House of God parties). He also sells DJ gear.

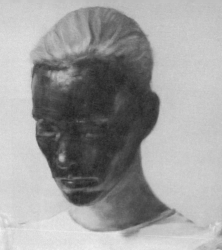

BO ZAR
EX PO

22.02 > 03.08.2014

Michaël
Borremans

As sweet as it gets

PALEIS VOOR
SCHONE KUNSTEN,
BRUSSEL

PALAIS
DES BEAUX-ARTS,
BRUXELLES

CENTRE
FOR FINE ARTS,
BRUSSELS

WWW.BOZAR.BE | + 32 (0)2 507 82 00

Michaël Borremans, The Angel, 2013, Courtesy Zeno X Gallery Antwerp © Dirk Pauwels

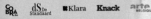

Is
Belo
or is
no

his
is
ium
this
t?

Nosedrip

25, was born and raised and Ostend and now lives in Ghent.
He is a DJ and founder of stroom.tv.

on Ostend

If you go to Ostend, don't go to the city beach. Take the KUSTTRAM along the shore, it stretches almost all the way between France and the Netherlands and has a great view. Close to where I grew up is the tram stop MARIAKERKE – this is where you should get off. There's a place called OLLIE'S POINT, a chilled-out spot where tourists don't go, just some surfers with their minivans. I used to go there a lot when I was 18. There's a good ice cream place nearby called GEORGE'S where my sister used to work. The lemon sorbet is nice. There are three Fritkots; one of them is called KENNY'S, it's the ugliest of them all but definitely the best, just a crappy green prefab that's been there forever. The portions are so big that two medium fries is enough for a whole family. There is not much in Ostend when it comes to art, even though it's the CITY OF JAMES ENSOR. His grave is close to Ollie's point in a very nice CEMETERY close to the dunes. Ostend is split in half by the HARBOUR and there's a boat that brings you to the industrial side of the harbour for free. It leaves every 15 minutes and is close to FORT NAPOLEON, a famous historic war site. I love the industrial area, there's such a nice vibe there. I think it's the best place in all of Ostend, but in about five years it will be gone. They're building new apartments there for rich people from Brussels and Antwerp. I saw the plans, they look terrible. There are still things left over from the fishermen: rusty metal, old boats, and a FISH MARKET with a photo series of fishermen by Belgian photographer STEPHAN VANFLETEREN on show. I think it's his best work. The exhibition wasn't meant to be permanent, but it is now. The images have been partly destroyed from the wind and salt, and it's a very special place. The best place to go out in Ostend is COPADOR, the first place I ever played. It's got a great atmosphere, and the beer is not that great but they try to do something a little different. It's very small and the sound is very good, which is an exception around here. The guy who works there has travelled all over the world, he's really cool and he's one of the only people from Ostend who knows what I'm doing and talks to me about it. He always has new songs on his iPod and is really up to date when it comes to music. During the day he selects the music and even in Ghent I can't think of a place where the selection is that good. OSTEND'S LIBRARY has a great music collection, something that played a big role in my life. There was this jazz musician from Ostend who gave his whole collection to the library after he died and it's just incredible. I borrowed so many CDs from there when I was 17 and 18, and I still play some tunes now that I discovered back then.

BIBLIOTHEEK KRIS LAMBERT
7 Wellingtonstraat (8400)

→
COPADOR
10 Langestraat (8400)

FORT NAPOLEON
Vuurtorenweg (8400)

GEORGES
15 Adolf Buylstraat (8400)

JAMES ENSOR'S GRAVE
Dorpstraat (8400)

KENNY'S
Sterstraat (8400)

VISSCHERSKOPPEN EXHIBITION
Oostendse Vismijn (8400)

Best for
live music

PETROL CLUB

25 d'Herbouvillekaai (2020)
petrolclub.be

Established in 1989, Petrol Club was started by the same people behind Ghent's Ten Days Off and is located in Antwerp's Zuid neighbourhood in an old industrial building (with a second, smaller place called Piaf next door). It hosts live bands and DJs covering dance, house, reggae, new wave and drum n' bass, from home and abroad (Hardcell, Grindvik, BMG, James Chance...) and the crowd is youngish and mostly local. The venue is a bit scruffy (one space with a capacity of 1,200) and dated in terms of sound, though there are plans to spruce it up.

TRIX

28-30 Noordersingel (2140)
trixonline.be

A firm Antwerp favourite since its 2004 opening, Trix's programme is classified as rock slash indie slash alternative, but it's well-known for its metal and hardcore gigs and dance events too. Many acts appear here way before they become famous (Band of Horses, M83, Yeasayer, Stromae...) and its three stages attract urbanites in their 20s and 30s. There are two annual festivals: Planet Caravan (psychedelics, doom, desert music) and We Are Open, a showcase festival for Belgians.

CACTUS

27 Magdalenastraat (8200)
cactusmusic.be

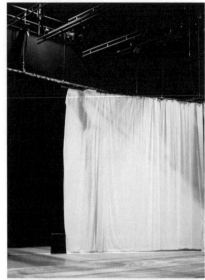

This community-funded association has been around since 1973, and in this particular location for 10 years. Purpose-built as a multidisciplinary arts centre (its architecture has won prizes), it's mostly just used for concerts. It's got one adaptable space that can fit up to 1,000 people, and the programme features a selection of ethnic, roots and electro music (it recently hosted Patti Smith, Sinéad O'Connor and Steve Earl).

LES ATELIERS CLAUS

15 Rue Crickxstraat (1060)
23 Rue de Brabantstraat (1210)
lesateliersclaus.com

It all started when Frans Claus began hosting get-togethers for artists in his Saint-Gilles / Sint-Gillis home studio back in the '90s. Today, his venue is considered *the* home of alternative and experimental music in Brussels. Railing against the "cultural standardisation" of concert venues, Claus and his team have opted instead for homey interiors and a programme filled with unheard-of arty-types including the likes of The Dead C and Matthieu Ha. It's recently undergone a makeover and now boasts two floors (150 downstairs, 100 upstairs), as well as a satellite venue in Rogier. Expect a loose atmosphere.

BEURSCHOUWBURG

20-28 Rue Auguste Ortsstraat (1000)
beursschouwburg.be

BONNEFOI

8 Rue des Pierres / Steenstraat (1000)
bonnefooi.be

A local institution since 1965, Beurschouwburg is housed in a 19th century ex-brewery that was renovated in 2004 by the architects behind La Monnaie/Muntpunt Opera. Thanks to neighbourhood noise complaints, gigs are now hosted on the fifth floor roof terrace (they used to be held on the ground floor), and it's a combination of up-and-comers and established acts. Punters are young – or young at heart – and often international while the atmosphere is low-key and genial. Some pretty big names passed through these doors early in their careers (U2, Tom Waits, Sisters of Mercy...) while recent visitors have included Planningtorock, Cold Cave and Sons of Disaster. It has a substantial programme of talks, lectures, projections and conferences on subjects ranging from visual identity and graphic design to cinema and politics and has also recently started hosting the Vinyl Market every first Thursday of the month.

Since 2008, Bonnefooi has been known as the place where nights come to an end, and is usually packed with bedraggled drinkers looking for "a last one." Roughly the size of a couple of living rooms, it can fit about 250 people at a time and is yet another city venue that tries to provide a platform for everybody and anybody. The sound quality suffers slightly as a result of the size and the squeeze, although it remains popular due to its good programming (local imprints On-Point Records and Onda Sonora host their Bedroom Beats series here).

BOTANIQUE
236 Rue Royale / Koningsstraat (1210)
botanique.be

BOZAR
23 Rue Ravensteinstraat (1000)
bozar.be

Botanique, Brussels' former botanical gardens, became a cultural centre for the French-speaking community in 1984. The Orangerie is the original building's biggest space (700 standing) while nearby satellite venue Cirque Royal can fit 2,000. About 50% of the acts are French-speaking Belgian up-and-comers while two of its most popular exports are Les Nuits Botanique festival, which takes place every year around the end of May, and Propulse, a showcase for Wallonia's burgeoning scene. Everyone from LIARS and Pavement's Stephen Malkmus to Danny Brown and Hercules & Love Affair have graced its stage. The sound is almost always impeccable and the greenery is a lovely little touch.

Bozar is an esteemed cultural institution and the national orchestra's HQ. An art deco masterpiece designed by Victor Horta, it hosts 250 concerts per year, and you're as likely to hear Italian arias as ska punk. There are countless arts and music festivals held throughout the year and the biggest space is Henry le Beouf Hall, which can hold up to 2,200. It hosts everything from Actress and Sewn Leather to the world's biggest and best symphony orchestras, as well as the Bozar Electronic Music Festival, a weekend-long showcase of both international and local talent.

DNA
18 Plattesteen (1000)
dnabxl.be

FLAGEY
1 Place Sainte-Croix
/ Heilig-Kruisplein (1050)
flagey.be

Ever since the '80s, DNA has been known as Brussels' premier headbangers' hangout with a penchant for punk – the city's very own CBGBs if you will. A dark baroque interior hides throngs of leather-clad ageing punks, adolescent emos and all the thirty-something new wavers in between, who come to see the likes of Casualties, Holograms, Warbringer, Arkangel and Tokyo Sex Destruction. Pre- or post-show drinking on the footpath outside the bizarre leopard-print facade is *de rigueur* where passersby are suitably terrified.

The listed art deco 'steamship' building that houses the Flagey cultural centre has a nice backstory: it used to be the country's radio and television HQ and, as such, has famously great acoustics. It's home to the Brussels Philharmonic Orchestra and gigs here tend to be on the grown-up side, with lots of classical and jazz and some contemporary listings thrown in, from The Romantics to Yuri Favorin and tributes to Marc Moulin. There are four rooms with a max capacity of 860, and Studio 4 has (perhaps) the best acoustics in the whole world.

MADAME MOUSTACHE
5-7 Quai au Bois à Brûler
/ Brandhoutkaai (1000)
madamemoustache.be

MAGASIN 4
51 Avenue du Port / Havenlaan (1000)
magasin4.be

This sweat-soaked 'neo-cabaret' is located in the tourist-thronged canal area of Place Sainte-Catherine/Sint-Katelijneplein. It's loud and trashy and comes replete with themed nights ('60s, '70s, sailors etc.) and while the atmosphere is very much the fashionable bohemia-chic you can find in many other bars, it's got quite the unique programme. More suited to live gigs, preferably with guitars, the calendar is full of the likes of Royal Canoe, Dead Gaze and Jonathan Toubin and it is also home to the city's best '60s rock nights, Back to the Grave, hosted by the guys behind local garage-rock outfit Mountain Bike. It's got one main dance floor, a smoking room and long lines after midnight.

Volunteer-run Magasin 4 is located in an industrial warehouse in Brussels' docklands. It's a little bit like DNA only bigger and, dare we say, better. They book hard rock, metal, hardcore and new wave (at the darker end) – no pop, rock or electro. The aim is to springboard artists from obscurity onto the local alternative scene, though they also book some better-knowns. In 19 years it's hosted more than 5,800 groups, including Bollock Brothers, Caspar Brotzman, Converge and Dub Trio. The location means it's a bit of a pain to get to, but cheap rent means cheap beer.

RECYCLART

25 Rue des Ursulinenstraat (1000)
recyclart.be

BRUSSELS

VK*

76 Rue de l'École / Schoolstraat (1080)
vkconcerts.be

BRUSSELS

The non-profit Recyclart, founded in 1997, is a neighbourhood multidisciplinary arts institution housed in a graffitied former train station. There are three live gigs per week held either in Studio Marcel or the main hall, which can hold about 600 people at a time. Acts are often local and often electronic with special attention paid to tropical bass, dubstep and avant-jazz, with recent bills including Blossoms and Futurs Morts. It also includes trade workshops for the unemployed, while the nearby railway underpasses function as urban open-air galleries.

When Vk* opened in 1989 it was on the cutting edge of alternative music in Brussels, booking key hip hop and indie acts way before they were cool (Rage Against The Machine's first Belgian appearance was a Vk*). These days, despite the appearance of so many venues in close proximity all gunning for the same up-and-coming bands (and that all-important community funding), Vk* continues to secure some of the hottest bookings in town (Ty Segall and Bishop Neru to name but two). At equal walking distance between Molenbeek's Etangs Noir / Zwarte Vijvers and Comte de Flandre / Graaf van Vlaanderen metro stations, the venue has a capacity of 600 and is known to also open its doors to local promoters and collectives (Belgian digital airwaves pioneer LDBK Radio will be celebrating its 12th birthday here on 22nd May for example).

4AD
57 Kleine Dijk (8600)
4ad.be

N9
165 Molenstraat (9900)
n9.be

DIKSMUIDE

EELKO

4AD first appeared in 1998 and is now in its third location in a former electrics warehouse, with a max capacity of 250. The programme doesn't concentrate on any one genre because it serves so much of the surrounding region that the programmers are required to be generalists. It attracts a crowd from both nearby and farther afield in Flanders who like the thrill of the unknown, and recent showings have included Motor Psycho, Girls Against Boys, Brussels Jazz Orchestra and Blautzen, to name but a varied few. Meg White once sold merchandise for her buddies who played here.

Founded in 1979 by a group of amateur enthusiasts, N9 gradually morphed into a professional music club that hosts everything from African, Latin, Caribbean music to folk and funk. Over the years it has welcomed the likes of Company Segundo, Desmond Dekker, Dr. John, Orchestre Baobab, Triggerfinger and Don Cherry. The audience is mixed and the atmosphere is cosy (100 seated, 200 standing), giving it the feeling of a professionally decked-out living room. The lead glass window designed by artist Ever Meulen is a nice touch. Helden in het Park is their (free) annual festival.

HANDELSBEURS
29 Kouter (9000)
handelsbeurs.be

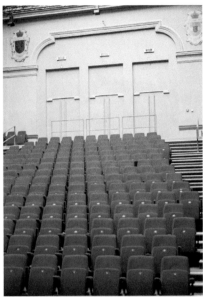

KINKY STAR
9 Vlasmarkt (9000)
kinkystar.be

Built in 1906, this restored baroque building was reopened to the public as a concert hall in 2002. Expect classical music, jazz, pop, rock, and flamenco, or events that combine all of the above (Kraakpand and Ha'fest). It prides itself on bridging gaps between genres, though the programme tends to attract a mostly jazzy, singer-songwritery, soul-loving crowd from the over-30 age bracket. The main concert hall can hold up to 850, and recent notables have included Joachim Badenhorst and the Chiaroscuro Quartet. Very civilised and centrally-located.

Kinky Star is a youth centre that has hosted more than 2,500 gigs since opening in 1997. A smallish venue, it books all kinds of alternative acts, and its programmer (also a member of Sexmachines and Starfighter and founder of the Kinky Star label) is famous for having his finger on the pulse of the Belgian and Flemish underground music scenes. Most of the groups are local, though they do look further afield, too (Band of Eli, The Guru Guru, Fabrieke, John Sinclair, Mon-O-Phone...) and most bands from Ghent have played its stage at one point or another in their career. Whatever's booming, they book it.

VOORUIT

23 Sint-Pietersnieuwstraat (9000)
vooruit.be

GHENT

MUZIEKODROOM

9 Bootstraat (3500)
muziekodroom.be

HASSELT

Vooruit is a household name in Ghent. It's located in a listed building – a former socialist meeting point – and was designated as an arts centre in 1982. The main hall can host 1,000 people and the programme features mostly contemporary concerts with a focus on adventurous guitar bands: from the experimental pop of Crooks on Tape, White Magic and Father Murphy, to the fingerpicking blues and folk of Steve Gunn and Cian Nugent. It also books underground electronica from the likes of Morphosis, Pete Swanson, Kaumwald and Felix Kubin and there's also a large popular café attached.

Hasselt's only venue worth mentioning is located in a former meat processing plant. Since the early '90s it's hosted alternative rock at the harder end of the scale, as well as indie soft pop guitar bands and a bit of electro, too (they're also really into the new generation of young electro rappers, like Yung Lean et al.) The venue fits about 1,000 and attracts a community of hard-partying students (for electro parties) while also acting as a focal point for Hasselt's underserved band scene. Their annual Play festival showcases a sampling of gigs hosted throughout the year.

DE KREUN
1 Conservatoriumplein (8500)
dekreun.be

KORTRIJK

HET DEPOT
12 Martelarenplein (3000)
hetdepot.be

LEUVEN

▲ stage

As Kortrijk's live music go-to venue since the early '80s, De Kreun doesn't focus on a single genre, opting instead for a mix of mainly new electronic, indie and psych. It's quite alternative and experimental, with bookings like Swans and Boombox, and popular with 30-something music purists. It's also famous for its annual Sonic City Festival, a two-day underground festival inspired by All Tomorrow's Parties, with alternating curators (Suuns, BEAK>, Liars, Millionaire...). The main space can hold up to 600.

This venue used to be a cinema before being converted into a gig venue by M10 architects and reopened in 2002. Like its contemporaries, Het Depot focuses on rock, albeit on the more soulful end of the spectrum. It books a lot of bands that are not so easy to pigeonhole, and virgin Leuven acts get a look in, as well as those that have already had some radio time. The biggest space in the venue can fit 850 at a time, and recent bookings have included Gary Numan, Heather Nova, Soulfly and the Robert Glaser Experiment. There are also instrument lessons and songwriting classes on offer.

L'ESCALIER
26 Rue Saint Jean-en-Isle (4000)

LIVE CLUB
13 Rue Roture (4020)
liveclubliege.be

Liège is the epicentre of rock in Wallonia (the world?) right now, thanks to great festivals and the endless parade of new bands it produces annually. Since opening 15 years ago, this venue has played a vital role in the development of the scene. Located in the district known as Le Carré, l'Escalier is a focal point for amateurs of rock and independent music in the region, and hundreds of local and international bands have graced its stage – everyone from Grandaddy, Dominique A and My Little Cheap Dictaphone to Girls in Hawaii, The Experimental Tropic Blues Band and Soldout, to name but a few. With just enough space for 200, it's rather on the squashed side.

This brand new venue rose from the ashes of Tipi, another popular Liège club, which itself was a reincarnation of Cirque d'hiver. Despite the changes to management and names, this place has been a feature on Liège's musical landscape for decades with an eclectic programme that has included DJ Vadim, Willie and the Bandits and Front 242. There are two spaces: Live Club with its sleek interior and good acoustics and space for 200, an upper floor and a big backstage area with a smoking section. Another space, Live Bar, can host up to 80.

LA ZONE
42 Quai de l'Ourthe (4020)
lazone.be

LIÈGE

BELVÉDÈRE
1 Avenue Marie d'Artois (5000)
belvedere-namur.be

NAMUR

This Outermeuse youth club started in 1991 in an old *liégeois* townhouse. The programme is open and experimental and features local and international acts that might find it difficult to fit in elsewhere. Rock, hip hop, punk, electro, cabaret and new burlesque fill the calendar, and the vibe is intimate (capacity 110). Programming is a collective affair, and past gigs have included such underground legends as UK Subs, Zion Train, Neurosis, Cornershop, Hyatus and Sham 69. It also hosts the annual 24h de Slam, the longest poetry open mic in the world.

Perched at the top of Namur, near the site of the annual Verdur Rock festival, the building that houses the Belvédère used to be the final stop for the cable car that brought visitors up to the city's iconic citadel. It was abandoned until 2007 when it got a shot in the arm in the form of city money, and these days it's one of the finest art and music institutions in the Walloon region. Run by a non-profit called Panama, the focus is pop and rock (Intergalactic Lovers, the Poneymen, Bombay Show Pigs...) but they also put on exhibitions and workshops and host artists in residence. That, plus the view is amazing.

NIJDROP
9 Kloosterstraat (1745)
nijdrop.be

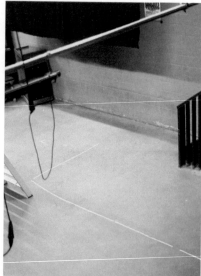

Founded in 1968, Nijdrop was Belgium's first
ever youth club. They've just built themselves
a brand new centre, a smallish venue with
two spaces, the biggest of which can fit up to
400 people. Thanks to their youth-oriented,
community-based origins, they are open in
terms of programming so everyone gets a
look in, and gigs cover a wide selection of
genres including hip hop, punk, electro, rock,
post-rock, drum n' bass, and swing (Marble
Sounds, Amenra, Novastar...) The crowd
is at the younger end of the scale with the
average age about 25.

CREATE EVERYTHING FROM NOTHING

RAFAEL GRAMPÁ, GRAPHIC NOVEL CREATOR, IS ONE OF FOUR INSPIRING
ARTISTS WHO HAVE TRANSFORMED THEMSELVES AND THEIR CREATIVE DISCIPLINE.

DISCOVER THEIR JOURNEY AT ABSOLUT.COM

ABSOLUT.
TRANSFORM TODAY

Please drink our know-how wisely

A weekend getaway at L'Ardoisière

L'Ardoisière is the name Pierre, Karl and Frédéric Huyghe have given to the dreamy haven of quiet they've created just under two hours by car from Brussels. Set on a sprawling three-hectare estate, the three brothers teamed up with architect friend Barbara Feret to transform the former slate mine's barns into a collection of six successive suites, each with their own theme and stunning views of the valley that extend beyond its front lawns. With an eye to making guests feel at home, all the food is cooked on site and served by Pierre, the youngest of three brothers who is always preceeded by his two dogs, Nina and Kiki. The place is ideal for parents and their kids, who'll love the swimming pool (built by the former owners in 1974 and replete with original artwork by Belgian artist Jean Dernat), 20 horses, six chickens (Justine, Mireille, Milène, Bip-Bip, Poulette and Nugets) and two cats (Georgette and Eugène). A family affair from start to finish, L'Ardoisière has established itself as the getaway of choice for the country's connoisseur creative classes, and rightly so.

compagniedesbois.be

Best for
vintage design

ATELIER SOLARSHOP
48 Dambruggestraat (2060)
ateliersolarshop.be

DESIGNGALLERY MARCY MICHAEL
78 Sint-Jozefstraat (2018)
marcymichael.com

Atelier Solarshop is a concept shop located in Antwerp's 2060 area that was founded in 2008 by Piëtro Celestina and Jan-Jan Van Essche. The name is a throwback to the days when the place served as a solar panel supplier. Much more than just a shop that sells stuff, it's also a kind of artistic hub that plays host to all kinds of events and exhibitions. Its eclectic selection includes vintage tables and chairs, fashion (including Jan-Jan's own line of clothes), art and jewellery.

Michael Marcy started collecting vintage pieces at the tender age of 21 and has become an expert over the years; some design addicts even refer to him as Belgium's design encyclopedia. He's especially dedicated to introducing collectors to Belgian architects and designers of the '40s and '50s and his legendary design gallery, located just outside Antwerp's city centre, has become a vintage design focal point of the city.

FULL EFFECT
63 Kloosterstraat (2000)
fulleffect.be

MODEST FURNITURE
247 Mechelsesteenweg (2018)
modestfurniture.com

Run by Carlo Westdorp, Full Effect is also located on Antwerp's antiques highway, Kloosterstraat. It's got furniture pieces, decorative items and great original gift ideas like hipster-friendly vintage radios. The shop's standout features are no doubt the extensive lamp section and the amazing collection of beautiful old professional racing bikes. He's also got second-hand threads for adults and kids – speaking of which, there's even a stockpile of vintage toys and barbies.

The goal of Modest Furniture is to promote, you guessed it, modest and positive design. Specialising in Danish and Scandinavian creations from the '50s, '60s and '70s, the collection includes everything from lighting and furniture to decoration. The shop is dotted with such design icons as an Eames Rar chair, Hove Møbler's blue daybed, and HP Hansen's teak sideboard. As an extra bonus, the shop also sells photographs of jazz musicians.

WOOD STOCK ANTIQUES

87 Kloosterstraat (2000)
woodstockantiques.be

Located in Kloostestraat in the heart of
Antwerp's antique quarter, Kris and Petra's
Wood Stock Antiques brings vintage
curiosities back from antiquity. They're
particularly known for their selection of
industrial furniture and bizarre items like old
leather gymnastic mats and sports balls. Fun
fact: they furnish none other than celebrated
fashion photographer Marc Lagrange with
props for his shoots.

AMPERSAND HOUSE

30 Rue de Suisse
/ Zwitserlandstraat (1060)
ampersandhouse.com

Run by Ike Udechuku and Kathryn Smith,
Ampersand House is located in a beautiful
old maison de maître in Saint-Gilles / Sint-
Gillis. It's a few things rolled into one: the
couple's home, a live-in gallery and a furniture
shop. Mixing vintage, contemporary and
prototype work, it's an interesting selection
where you'll find everything from Grete Jalk's
gorgeous teak armchairs to Bernt Petersen's
Egyptian stools.

D+ DESIGN
83 Rue Blaesstraat (1000)
dplusdesign.be

INFLUENCES
44 Rue Darwinstraat (1050)

Italian-born Allessandro Dati has a passion for 20th century furniture and decorative lighting, with an obvious preference for Italian design. The shop, located on Brussels' antiques high street Rue Blaes, stocks creations by such post-war design godfathers as Gio Ponti, Ettore Sottsass and Joe Colombo, as well as a few Scandinavian, European and American pieces. You'll no doubt be particularly enamoured by the many different kinds of Guzzini lamps.

Founded by Pierre De Brouwere and Beatrice Cousin a few years back, this little jewel in the vintage-loaded Brugmann neighbourhood is a furniture shop-cum-art gallery. The carefully-arranged elegant space and selection are the work of true passionates whose particular specialty is Belgian contemporary abstract art and Scandinavian and Belgian furniture pieces from the '50s, '60s and '70s.

LE PETIT COIN

2 Rue Antoine Labarrestraat (1050)
lepetitcoin.be

MOBILIÈRE XXe

65 Rue de la Régence
/ Regentschapsstraat (1000)
olibil.com

Olivier Biltereyst's Mobiliere XXe is located in the Grand Sablon / Grote Zavel, Brussels' upmarket antiques quarter. The shop buys and sells elegant and sophisticated bits and pieces of 20th century furniture for design addicts, mostly French and Italian pieces, and a part of the space has been dedicated to selling art books – a little enterprise run by Laurent Bouchat.

Located in the Flagey area and run by three friends, newcomer Le Petit Coin is a funky little corner shop that opens Thursdays, Fridays and Saturdays (and by appointment). It's no bargain basement, but it's got some choice finds for the smaller wallet. Apart from furniture, it's full of little bits and pieces from cushions, plates, cups and lots of different deco objects but – fair warning – not everything here is vintage.

VIA ANTICA
40 Rue Blaesstraat (1000)
antiek.net/viaantica

VINTAGE ITEMS
33 Rue Darwinstraat (1050)

Located in the bohemian Marolles / Marollen quarter of Brussels, this gigantic space is the Goliath of Belgium's vintage design scene. Covering 2,000 square metres and three floors, Via Antica unites 40 different dealers covering a whole array of different styles and a wide range of pieces from the 18th to the 20th centuries. You can find '70s Scandinavian masterpieces alongside art deco lamps and ancient pharmacy shelves. It's a treasure trove of design gems, one that goes on and on and on.

Vintage Items, again located in the Brugmann neighbourhood, is notable for the colourful selection of multi-coloured lettering taken from vintage signage that decorates the walls, as well as a horde of knick-knacks from the '60s to the '80s. Owner Tim Dubus always has some grand classics out on display, from Marcel Breuer chairs to pieces by Eames and Jacobsen.

DEPOT 09
118 Nieuwevaart (9000)
depot09.be

OH LES BEAUX JOURS
48 Rue des Franchimontois (4000)
ohlesbeauxjours.be

Depot 09 is a relative newcomer on Belgium's vintage design route having only opened in 2013, but it's already set to be one of the country's best addresses. Bringing together dealers from Belgium and the Netherlands, the former depot along the water outside Ghent's city centre is big in size and eclectic in selection. It's a beautiful spot, with an exposed brick wall and floor and a selection of art books for sale with comfy beanbags for your reading pleasure.

Former RTBF journalist André Leruth (who's also the driving force behind Liège's Vintage Days) opened this lovely shop when he retired. The focus is on design from the '60s to the '80s, but a few fitting pieces from other decades have managed to find their way into his selection, too. The range includes everything from vintage radios and ceramics to all kinds of furniture, lamps and phones, and it scores top marks for friendly prices.

Marie Pok

40, was born in Uccle / Ukkel and now lives in nearby Forest / Vorst.
She is the artistic director of Grand Hornu in Mons.

on Wallonia & Brussels' design scenes

The region of Hainaut is undergoing a kind of second life right now.
There's suddenly a big focus on culture, especially in Charleroi and
Mons, which is set to become the European Capital of Culture in 2015.
Up until a few years ago there were more design shops in Liège than
in Brussels and it's only because so many new places have opened in
Brussels that it overtook Liège. Of course Liège has always been very
important on both a local and European level, particularly thanks to the
month-long LIÈGE DESIGN TRIENNIAL (the next edition of which
runs in October 2015). There are a number of very important addresses
in the field of design; I particularly like LES DRAPIERS, a very small
textiles gallery whose focus sits somewhere between art and design.
It's very conceptual and run by a lady who used to be a textile design
teacher. The WCC in Mons is also very well-regarded: it's a centre
for applied arts located in a former abattoir and they exhibit ceramic
art, glasswork and jewellery, and they have two or three biennials that
are unmissable. But it's true that Brussels is the design capital of the
country right now. So many design spaces have opened in the city in
recent years, such as LA FABRIKA and DITTO, and many new
vintage design boutiques. I really like MA, which is an initiative of a
furniture designer called MARINA BAUTIER who makes everything
in her workshop-cum- shop. It's a new economic model that allows
designers to cut out the middleman. It's so good for designers to be
free, to produce, sell and distribute themselves. It's all in the DIY spirit,
and a result of the current economic situation. Does the result suffer
as a result of all this freedom? It's a risk. Without critical distance,
without a curator, you can have very bad design. It's also an invitation
to produce too much waste, to just produce for the sake of it, and there
will come a saturation point. I find it really bizarre and unfortunate
that Brussels has no public collection of contemporary art. WIELS
and other centres like it have to borrow their pieces. There used to be
a national collection in the Royal Museum of Modern Art but it was
closed for works and the director decided not to reopen it, so most of
the works are in storage. Instead, he opened a fin de siécle 19th century
museum. Many in the art world were, and still are, shocked. Likewise,
there is no place exclusively dedicated to graphic art in Brussels.
There is currently a project – a Contrat de Quartier – that has sprung
up in response to the derelict 17th century ABBAYE DE FOREST.
It's beautiful but it's more or less in ruins. I want to be part of the
regeneration project because I'd love to see it used as some kind of
cultural centre, and there are a number of creatives in Forest/Vorst
who are campaigning to get something done with the site, and my idea
would be to do something around graphic design.

ABBAYE DE FOREST
9 Place Saint-Denis /
Sint Denijsplein (1190)

DITTO
62 Rue de l'Aurore
Dageraadstraat (1000)

→
LA FABRIKA
182 Rue Antoine
Dansaertstraat (1000)

LES DRAPIERS
68 Rue Hors Château
(4000) Liège

MA
314 Chausée De Forest /
Vorstsesteenweg (1190)

WCC
17/02 Rue de la Trouille
(7000)

Dieter Van Den Storm

36, was born in Brussels, where he still lives.
He is design curator at Bozar.

on Brussels' North district

I moved to this neighbourhood because I heard the Flemish architect EUGEEN LIEBAUT was working on his first and only work in Brussels, the LIMMART building, and I immediately looked it up. I was lucky; there was still one apartment left and I took it right away. There are lots of nice buildings around here, including the high-rise AMELINCKX buildings and the CITROEN GARAGE, built back in the '30s when cars were still a luxury product. All the buildings were part of 'the Manhattan Plan' for the area around North Station; it was supposed to be a little New York. Everything is changing around here, but gradually. I've been living in Brussels for 12 years now and I've stopped being naïve. You always think things are changing, and they are, but it takes a lot of time. Just look at the CANAL / KANAL ZONE, look how long it's taking. I welcome these changes because they make the neighbourhood a more social place. Not so long ago, local entrepreneur Frédéric Nicolay opened the FLAMINGO BAR here and it's really good for the neighbourhood because it brings people together. We used to have to go all the way to the centre to have a drink, there were no nice bars, no cafés, just some bars where the hookers and transvestites go. I don't want to put pressure on Flamingo bar, but its arrival was so important for the neighbourhood and brought about a very notable change. It's a place where people meet, where you can see your neighbours outdoors, and not only in the hallway of your building. The presence of the hookers creates a strange atmosphere: it reminds me of the movies of Spanish director Pedro Almodovar. The only place to eat around here is BAR BIK, it's rather small with a lot of wooden benches and nice lighting. They try to be innovative with traditional Flemish dishes and the menu is great. The interior reminds me a bit of the Flamingo bar – both are cosy but at the same time young and contemporary. A lot of people go there for lunch meetings or for a snack before going to the theatre at eight; Brussels' three major theatres are nearby – the NATIONAL THEATRE, KAAITHEATER and the KVS. Behind the Flemish theatre there's an installation called CEMENT TRUCK by Belgian artist Wim Delvoye; a big truck made out of metal pieces from cathedrals. It's amazing. Also, there's a real animal farm called FERME DU PARC MAXIMILIEN in front of the Citroen Garage on a former helicopter landing port. Most people think it's just a park but there are donkeys, chicken, goats... Once I was sitting in my living room and there was no traffic and all of a sudden I saw a sheep run down the street! I think it's for school kids, some kind of city project to teach children where milk comes from. In the summer when it's hot you have this typical farm smell which is funny to have in a city.

BAR BIK
3 Quai aux Pierres
de Taille /
Arduinkaai (1000)

FERME DU PARC
MAXIMILIEN
21 Quai du Batelage /
Schipperijkaai (1000)

FLAMINGO BAR
171 Rue de Laeken /
Lakensestraat (1000)

KAAITHEATER
11 Square Sainctelette /
Saincteletteesquare (1000)

LIMMART APARTMENTS
33 Avenue de l'Héliport /
Helihavenlaan (1000)

NATIONAL THEATRE
111 Boulevard Emile
Jacqmainlaan (1000)

WIM DELVOYE STATUE
40 Quai au Foin /
Hooikaai (1000)

Charly Wittock

46, is the founder of AWAA, a Brussels-based architecture firm.
He was born in Italy.

on Brussels landmarks

Someone told me that they went to PARKING 58 recently and the rooftop was closed. I'm not sure what's happening, but I wouldn't be surprised if they tore it down. They've shamelessly demolished all of Brussels' coolest buildings from the '60s. I often bring visitors to Parking 58. I could take them to the PALAIS DE JUSTICE/JUSTITIEPALEIS, where the view is exceptional, but it's only 180° and that's where the tourists go. At Parking 58 you get 360°. I drive them up to the roof and I show them the city. I point things out to them, or sometimes we just sit there in the car. It's an interesting modernist building, kind of dirty and a little bit trashy. If they decided to tear it down tomorrow, I wouldn't be surprised. One of my favourite buildings was the futuristic Martini tower in PLACE ROGIER, which was demolished and replaced with an uninteresting block of offices. It's all about money, and the Bruxelloise – itself a very open concept – know this and can joke about it. It might not be the most beautiful place but there's a lot of originality in this city. There's not as much hype (or as much talent) as big cities like New York or London, but it's the coolness, the cynicism, the irony, the quirkiness that attract me. There's a place I know, run by a guy called Jean Marchetti, a hairdresser from a migrant Italian family. He was always interested in art but he never went to school. He transformed his little hair salon into a gallery called LE SALON D'ART in Saint-Gilles/Sint-Gillis, which has become quite a cool neighborhood. I never have much time, so I go there to get my hair cut and check out some art. Places like that have always interested me. In the DANSAERT DISTRICT there's a restaurant called the LE SELECTO where you can eat in the kitchen while watching the chef at work, if you want. I love being able to do that. I love cooking, and I love eating and actually, the best way to get to know a city is by getting names of all the good restaurants – you'll find that there are often interesting places to see on the way. Next to Le Selecto is a great place called ALICE GALLERY, one of the first galleries for graphic art, and right behind that is a kid's theatre called the BRONKS in a cool contemporary building. So you see? Go eat at the Le Selecto, then you come across Alice, then you see the Bronks, and then you have the Dansaert neighbourhood right next to it with all its cool clothes shops. There's a great company called D-TOURS who make downloadable city tours; you put your headphones on and a voice guides you, telling you to turn left, to stop, go right, go into a bar, to go out... It's like going to the movies except you're the hero. There's one on CONTEMPORARY ARCHITECTURE IN MOLENBEEK, all these amazing buildings you normally wouldn't even see, and the one of the MAROLLES has interviews with very ancient people talking about how it's been gentrified. It's one of the most amazing experiences I've ever had, and a great way to get to know Brussels. It's true that this is not the world's most beautiful city, but things here don't need to be especially beautiful to be beautiful, if you see what I mean?

ALICE GALLERY
4 Rue du Pays de Liège /
Land Van Luikstraat (1000)

BRONKS
15 Varkensmarkt /
Marché au Porc (1000)

D*Tours
d-tours.org

PALAIS DU JUSTICE
1 Place Poelaertplein
(1000)

PARKING 58
1 Rue de l'Evêque /
Bisschopstraat (1000)

LE SALON D'ART
81 Rue de l'Hôtel des
Monnaies /
Munthofstraat (1060)

LE SELECTO
95 Rue de Flandre /
Vlaamsesteenweg, (1000)

SHOES ARE BORING
WEAR SNEAKERS

THE CONVERSE CHUCK TAYLOR ALL STAR TIE-DYE SNEAKER

★ CONVERSE

Belgium's street artists

Although the local police precinct would probably disagree, neighbourhoods wouldn't be neighbourhoods without the odd graffiti-covered wall, oversized stencil or subtle sticker. Truth is, street artists are today finally being recognised as being integral parts to the communities they "serve," their works now seen as natural extensions of the urban décor we all live in, one of the many elements that define a particular district's character. Refusing to remain neutral and simply stay put when confronted with the country's many greying surfaces, these creative souls bring shots of colour where they are needed the most, embellishing their cities with unparalleled determination and unrestricted urban wizardry. In close collaboration with long-term partners Converse, whose support of the artistic community involves providing them with prime blank canvases to colour-splash, we sat down with some of the country's most prolific public art protagonists to get them talking about the cities, streets and walls they colour.

Visit thewordmagazine.com/ThisIsBelgium/StreetArtists for images of the artists' collaboration with Converse.

Cities need graffiti in their streets, otherwise they're dead. Belgium really needs a lot of colour, there are so many grey, ugly walls. I paint a lot in abandoned places and I try to find walls that are still completely clean and free of tags so that I can play with little details such as a red door for example. I live in Brussels and pay a lot of attention to its architecture. I'm sure that Horta and all that influenced me quite a bit. I love colour, it's very important to my art – I particularly like the really flashy neon colours. I prefer painting in the street because I want to share what I do and make people see it. Plus, graffiti is a lot about the social component and meeting people. My compositions are very abstract and full of organic forms. They're all based on music and rhythm. I never paint without my headphones. The music defines the lines and forms that I paint. I listen to everything but sometimes I give myself constraints by listening only to one style, like metal or hip hop. According to the musical style, the paintings vary a lot. It's all very spontaneous.

I started painting around the age of 14 but stopped after a while because I got into too much trouble with the police. I grew up in a little town in Limburg and it was too easy to get caught. Later I moved to Antwerp to study art at the Royal Academy and started painting walls again. The scene in Antwerp was much bigger of course, but I always felt like an outsider because I didn't grow up there. I don't want to do damage in the city centers and love to paint in abandoned places where I make 70% of my art. I find them by checking on Googlemaps. Some of them, like this one here in Mechelen, I basically use as a studio. I can take my time and try things. I make about 120 pieces a year, two walls a week. I don't just try to fill walls, I try to integrate my bugs and birds into them. I particularly like walls which are imperfect and have character. They need to have lived for a while. I use a lot of colours, not only for me, but also for the people. It gives a much more positive vibe. I'm actually colour-blind so in art school they told me I could never make art, but I proved them wrong.

I discovered graffiti when I was about 12 years old. I made my parents drive me around so I could look at walls and highway bridges. I grew up in Knokke-Heist where there wasn't much of a scene. Even today there are just two of us. The first time I took up a spray can was in an old abandoned swimming pool, which has now been replaced by fancy apartments. My first attempts were not good but I was instantly hooked. It became an obsession. I was always making sketches, my school books were full of them. I must have made thousands. But now I mostly paint freestyle, without sketches. Knokke really needs some more colour and we are trying to convince the city to let us paint some big walls. It is hard to describe a good wall: when you see it, you just feel it. When I am outside I constantly check around for walls I could paint on. Belgium still needs a lot of colour, although it's already getting better. I love colours, to think about how to combine them and to play around with them. A good artist can already do something with just a few colours. They make people happy.

I got into graffiti in the mid '80s through the hip hop movement from the US. It was a whole new culture that arrived back then. Once I saw someone spraying the outlines of a letter in a Malcom McLaren music video, I knew I wanted to do that. It was this video which made me pick up a spray can for the very first time, and I was instantly hooked. I can't explain it. It just feels magical. In the beginning we all just copied and imitated other artists. The New York scene was a big influence and pioneering books such as Subway Art and Spraycan Art were our bibles.

Marvel and DC comics were influences too. I find walls by walking around with open eyes and by word of mouth. I almost exclusively paint in abandoned places, because I can do whatever I want. When you do commissions there are too many rules and concessions. I love walls that are a bit ravaged, where you can really see the material and play with it. I like it when it has volume. And I try to make stuff which is timeless and classical. Colours are very important to create contrasts and really need to cry out... it's a science and you never stop learning.

DEFO
BRUSSELS

BUE
GHENT

I am from the north of Brussels, where the graffiti scene originated. I started painting around 1992. At the time you were considered a bit of a gangster when you did graffiti. I got picked on in school and graffiti allowed me to express myself without having to show my face. I paint in abandoned places a lot, but people don't really get to see it there. The advantage is that you can paint 16 hours in a row and not have to worry about getting caught. My favourites are old tile walls. I like it when walls have different surfaces and textures in them: small and big bricks, windows and little holes. I play with these elements and unify everything in my compositions. Colours are very important to me. I use powerful and intense colours because they bring the wall alive – but also because you need to catch people's attention. We paint to make the cities nicer, but you're not recognised by the city. Only when you get famous abroad and represented by a gallery, then they love you all of a sudden and stop destroying your stuff. It really hurts when they paint over my works. But that's normal, all street art is temporary.

For me graffiti was never about the adrenalin kick or trying to access dangerous or forbidden places. I'm not into that. I paint for the public, to make our surroundings nicer, happier and more colourful. Belgium definitely needs a lot of colour. Colour makes people happy. There's no sex and crime in my paintings, it's all quite positive, stuff that children like too. Lots of graffiti artists paint in abandoned buildings, but I'm not really into that because people won't see it. I want to reach as many people as possible. I've had exhibitions in Mexico City and LA, but that's not really what graffiti is about. It's supposed to be for the public and improve the city, not to be put away in a room where only a few people will notice it. I feel part of the neighbourhood where I live in Ghent, and I've already painted more than a few walls there. I definitely want to make my neighbourhood nicer. When I see a nice wall on a private house that I would love to paint on, I ring the doorbell and ask the owner and sometimes they say yes. Usually if one person says yes in the neighbourhood the others do too.

Belgium's hidden celebrity sightings

BENOÎT POELVOORDE'S FAVOURITE DINNER TABLE

Part of the Niels family's small empire of timeless restaurants (whose founder, Joseph Niels, famously invented L'Americain, Belgium's delicacy dish of raw minced meat mixed with egg yolk in 1929), the Canterbury sits on the edge of the city's stunning Etangs d'Ixelles, its terrace one of the area's best when the sun comes out. It is also celebrated Belgian actor Benoît Poelvoord and director Stefan Liberski's favourite dig, a fact cemented in style with a small, golden nameplate affixed to the wall of their favourite table.

MARVIN GAYE'S OSTEND PAD

In 1981, Marvin Gaye left the United States for Ostend in a bid to escape the hold drugs and women had on his life at the time. He stayed in the coastal city for two years, and went onto pen his last album "Sexual Healing" which won him a Grammy in 1983. During his two-year stint, this is the apartment building he called home.

AUDREY HEPBURN'S BRUSSELS BIRTHPLACE

In the backstreets of Brussels' Matonge area, a couple of houses up from L'Epicerie, one of the city's best lunchtime eateries, sits the birthplace of cinematic icon Audrey Hepburn, who was born at 48 Rue Keyenveldtsraat on 4th May 1929. A nameplate on the left of the townhouse's entrance serves as testament.

What the people really want

Truth be told, Brussels hasn't always enjoyed the best of reputations when it comes to good old retail therapy. Grumpy shop assistants, uninspiring displays, limited choice and a lack of professionalism were all criticisms often levelled at the city's retail operators. And, in a world of fast-paced change led by the advent of e-commerce and customers' own higher expectations, something simply needed to be done to help the city's high streets regain their chutzpah. In steps regional trade agency Atrium, who asked over 12,000 local customers a few questions in order to find out what is it they really want out of their shopping experience. Here, we partner up with the local agency to illustrate what came out of the study. Call them the four hidden rules of retail excellence as handpicked by you, the customer.

Proximity

The precinct needs to embody the community it serves. Customers want to recognise themselves in their neihgbourhood's shopping quarters and spend their hard-earned cash in places where everyone knows their name. They want a butcher, a baker, a hairdresser, a locksmith, a cobbler, a local bar and maybe a restaurant or two. Underscoring a deep sense of attachment to their local high street, they want a neighbourhood with a soul, a shopping community with defined values and distinctive visions.

Professionalism

The service needs to be on-point. Think shop assistants with a human feel, a passion for what they sell and some well-placed knowledge about the products on their shelves. Far removed from the anonymous and distant experience of online shopping, customers expect tailored advice when walking through the door. They want authenticity and a return to the "Client is king" motto.

Presentation

The neighbourhood needs to be inviting. Think wide pedestrian lanes, designated parking areas, rows upon rows of trees (we'd go for Japanese cherry trees), distinctive urban furniture (preferably made out of local timber by the precinct's design academy students), striking window displays and just a touch of community appeal. Improving the community's daily lives, through a combination of comfort, originality and distinctive aesthetics, must remain priority number one.

Products

The shelves need to dazzle. Customers want to be caught off-guard, they want surprise and have the feeling they're being told and shown something before the others. Put simply, products should be LATTE: Local, authentic, traceable, trusted and ethical.

Devrim Bayar

33, is residency programme curator at WIELS and founder of Le Salon. She was born and raised in Brussels.

on Brussels' contemporary art scene

Brussels has become the centre of contemporary art in Belgium. There are more and more curators and artists arriving, more and more small art projects setting up, more and more galleries opening a first or a second space here. I just hope it doesn't become saturated like Berlin. When I travel I often hear people talking about Brussels the way people used to talk about Berlin, and it's true that rent has been rising and local artists are having a harder time finding places to work. But when you compare it with Amsterdam or Paris, it's still pretty cheap. WIELS was the first big contemporary art centre project in the city but now there are alternatives, such as LA LOGE. For me, HARALD THYS and MARGOT VANHEUSDEN, a couple who manage the artist-run space Etablissement d'en face, are emblematic of the current Brussels scene. Harald works with another artist called Jos de Gruyter and they are my favourite artist duo. ÉTABLISSEMENT D'EN FACE was the first artist-run space in Brussels and has been around for 20 years, and the art community gathers there en masse. Harald and Margot have the ability to attract artists and the art world. They live above a little kitsch Turkish family café on Rue de Flandre / Vlaamsesteeneweg called MIDPOINT, which doubles as their local. People in the art world started to go there, and it is now the café for artists – not collectors! – to meet. There are other cafés that are known for attracting artists, such as DARINGMAN or CHEZ MARTINE, also on Rue de Flandre / Vlaamsesteeneweg, but more and more artists find themselves at Midpoint. Not far from there is a small gallery called DÉPENDANCE, which has a very nice roster of artists including some of my favourites, like Thomas Bayrle and Jana Euler. The director himself is a trained artist which means he has a rapport with the artists he represents. Another project I find very original is the relatively-unknown DE AVONDEN, which are soirees in which an artist is invited to talk about their work. Often, it takes place in cafés and is really informal. They've already had really well-known international artists as well as locals, and there is no website, no Facebook page or archive, there is simply a mailing list, because they want to keep the meetings intimate. It's a good time to be an artist in Brussels. As a city it's never been known for its charisma, and the weather is known for being shit all year. Brussels' image is the opposite of glamour, unlike Berlin with its clubbers and rich history. That's why I really like the HOLLYWOOD SIGN by Gregory Decock and Pierre De Belgique; it's ironic. They pretended to be painters to get access to the building, you can see it from Place Poelaertplein. For me it's a kind of statement that sums up what Brussels is about.

CHEZ MARTINE
37 Rue de Flandre /
Vlaamsesteenweg (1000)

DÉPENDENCE
4 Rue Du Marché aux
Porcs / Varkensmarkt
(1000)

ÉTABLISSEMENT
D'EN FACE
32 Rue Ravensteinstraat
(1000)

LA LOGE
86 Rue de l'Ermitage
/ Kluisstraat (1050)

→
MIDPOINT
189 Rue de Flandre
Vlaamsesteenweg (1000)

Murielle Scherre

36, is the founder of La Fille D'O,
a Ghent-based lingerie brand.

on Ghent

People from Ghent tend to wander but they always come back. I don't
really know why. People from other places move to new cities and new
countries and never go home. But people always come back to Ghent.
It's small enough to make you want to leave but also small enough
that you can come back and make your mark – which gives the place
a special atmosphere. And because it's so small it doesn't have hype
neighbourhoods like in Brussels or Antwerp. In Ghent, gentrification
happens at street level. It's happening on our street, BURGSTRAAT.
About four years ago there was nothing really going on here, just a
couple of old antique shops. Now, there's an architect's studio, as well
as LE JARDIN BOHÉMIEN, a pop-up shop slash vintage store slash
café slash B&B... run by an interior architect and his wife. I'm not really
into concept stores – nowadays anybody can do it – but these guys have
about 50 million concepts going on at once. I like that, I like people who
are serious and who are good at what they do. I hate hype. That was
the worst thing about my brand when we started out: we caused a riot
because there's not much happening in lingerie-land. But now that we've
been around for 10 years, well it's hard to be hype for 10 years. Up-and-
coming brands often create hype so things progress quickly – but then
they disappear. It's a kind of natural selection. OORCUSSEN is a
high-end fashion store that's been around for 20 years – it was the first
store in Ghent to stock all the Belgian designers. I have a lot of respect
for the owner because she educated an entire generation here and she's
still doing it, she never lost her touch. Her store was never just about
hype. I don't like brand stores or flagship stores, it's all fluff and no
substance. Similarly there's a little restaurant I love called LEPELBLAD
that makes the best food; their menu is always changing and the staff
are incredible. There are so many restaurants that put a lot of work into
their logo and branding and seating and décor, and then the food arrives
and it's only so-so. These guys keep a low profile but their food is the
best, and I love them for that. I'm quite militant about authenticity. I'm
really into valuable things, and by that I don't mean expensive things,
but things that are well-made or that were fashionable once. There's a
place called the VERKOOPZAAL in the up-and-coming MUIDE area
in the north of Ghent, a huge warehouse where they take valuable items
that have been thrown away and return them to their rightful status: as
beautiful, valuable objects. It's all very selective. Normally these shops
are very crappy and they take everything they are offered, but the owner
is very critical. My flat is full of stuff from there. And just around the
corner from my street is a bookshop called THE BLIND TRAVELLER
run by this mad-professor kind of guy and my studio is filled with his
beautiful art books from there. I've built walls in my office with them.
It's a magical selection, but I try not to go there because I've got way
too much stuff. I have a lot of respect for things once they're made. I like
things with a story and I've often thought: how cool would it be to be
able to talk to things?

→

LE JARDIN BOHÉMIEN
19 Burgstraat (9000)

OORCUSSEN
7 Vrijdagmarkt (9000)

LEPELBLAD
40 Onderbergen (9000)

THE BLIND TRAVELLER
45 Burgstraat (9000)

MURIELLE SCHERRE

Best
for fountains
in Brussels

Flagey (1050)

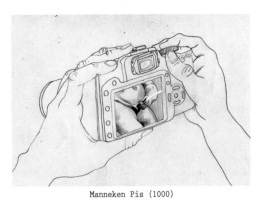

Manneken Pis (1000)

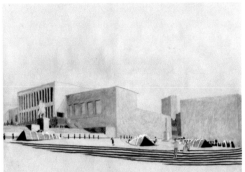

Place de l'Albertine / Albertinaplein (1000)

Mont des Arts / Kunstberg (1000)

Quai aux Briques / Baksteenkai (1000)

Montgomery (1150)

Vieux Marché aux Grains / Oude Graanmarkt (1000)

Place Fontainasplein (1000)

Place Dailly / Daillyplein (1030)

Place du Petit Sablon / Kleine Zavel (1000)

Les Jardins Botanique / De Kruidtuin (1210)

Here, there and everywhere

Citadelpark, Ghent

The Arboretum, Tervuren

Rivierenhof, Antwerp

Boelaerpark, Antwerp

Les Bains du Centre, Brussels

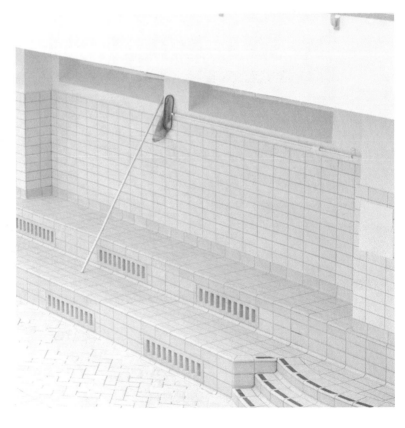

Le Paradis des Enfants, Etterbeek

The playground at Georges Henri park, Woluwe-Saint-Lambert / Sint-Lambrechts-Woluwe

Playground at Porte de Hal, Saint-Gilles / Sint-Gillis

This is Belgium is a project of
The Word Magazine.

Editor-in-chief and artistic director
 Nicholas Lewis

Editor
 Rose Kelleher

Design
 PLMD (pleaseletmedesign)

Writers
 Rose Kelleher
 Nicholas Lewis
 Sarah Schug

Photographers
 Jef Claes
 Joke De Wilde
 Sarah Eechaut
 Miles Fischler
 Veerle Frissen
 Lisa Lapierre
 Sarah Michielsen
 Grégoire Pleynet
 Anne Richards
 Tatiana Soumar

Illustrator
 Ida Michel

Print
 Bema Graphics

Distribution
 Exhibitions International

Publisher
 Jam Publishing sprl
 107 Rue General Henrystraat
 (1040) Belgium

First English edition published in 2014.
© 2014 Jam Publishing / The Word

This book would not have been possible
without the additional help and support of
the following people:

Marie Annaert, Devrim Bayar, Alasdair Bell,
Benoit Berben, Bruno Brunet, Jergan
Callebaut and Dalai Lama Records,
Diane Cappuyns, Alex Deforce and
On-Point Records, Pieter De Kegel,
Geoffroy Delobel, Ziggy Devriendt aka DJ
Nosedrip, Adrien Domken, Delphine Dupont,
Céline Fouarge, Julien Fournier and
Vlek Records, David Gelfius, Jane Haessen
of Catclub, Dimitri Jeurissen, Cynthia Lewis,
Jessie Lewis, Simon McDermott,
Pauline Miko, Philippe Pourhashemi,
Baptiste Péron, Emilie Pisscheda,
Gioia Seghers, Yassin Serghini, Bart Sibiel
and Onda Sonora, Charline Stoelzaed,
Pauline Testa, Géraldine Van houte,
Peter von Grumme, David Widart

Back cover © Joke De Wilde

ISBN 9789082215007
D/2014/13.423/1

This is Belgium
is also available
as an iPhone app
↓

Mu.ZEE,
the art museum
by the sea
Ostend

Mu.ZEE features a unique collection of Belgian art from 1830 to the present day, making it a one-of-a-kind museum in Flanders.

The collections are presented on a rotating basis and the museum has adopted an active exhibition policy reflecting the trends on the international art scene. Moreover, Mu.ZEE has a rich visitors' and activities programme, making Romestraat 11 a lively cultural haven!

Discover the **Léon Spilliaert** wing or the masterpieces wing where you can admire works by **James Ensor**, **Roger Raveel**, **Marcel Broodthaers**, **Luc Tuymans** and many others. And don't forget to drop by Mu.ZEE's satellite museums: the Permeke Museum in Jabbeke, which houses some 80 paintings by **Constant Permeke**, virtually his entire sculptural oeuvre and many large drawings; and the **James Ensor** House in Ostend, where the artist himself once lived!

Mu.ZEE
Romestraat 11
B-8400 Ostend
Tuesday–Sunday: 10 am – 6 pm
Closed on Mondays, 25.12 & 1.1
info@muzee.be
www.muzee.be

Mu.
ZEE

Kunstmuseum
aan zee
Collecties van
de Provincie
West-Vlaanderen en
de Stad Oostende

west-vlaanderen de gedreven provincie

OOSTENDE

If I told you I was Belgian, you probably
wouldn't believe me.